*i*Village
Solutions™

THE FRUGAL WOMAN'S
Guide to a Rich Life

STACIA RAGOLIA

EDITOR

Rutledge Hill Press®
Nashville, Tennessee

A Division of Thomas Nelson, Inc.
www.ThomasNelson.com

Other *i*Village Solutions Books

Best Advice on Finding Mr. Right

Best Advice on Life After Baby Arrives

Best Advice on Starting a Happy Marriage

Heirloom Recipes

Quiz Therapy

Six Weeks to Losing It for Good

Published by Rutledge Hill Press, a Division of Thomas Nelson, Inc., P.O. Box 141000, Nashville, Tennessee 37214.

Library of Congress Cataloging-in-Publication Data

The frugal woman's guide to a rich life / Stacia Ragolia, editor.
    p. cm. — (iVillage Solutions)
  Includes index.
  ISBN 1-4016-0103-0 (pbk.)
  1. Women-Finance, Personal. 2. Consumer education. 3. Home economics.
 I. Ragolia, Stacia, 1968– II. Series.
HG179.F78 2003
332.024'0082—dc22   2003015084

Printed in the United States of America
03 04 05 06 07 — 5 4 3 2 1

CONTENTS

— ◆ —

ACKNOWLEDGMENTS

———— ✦ ————

Since iVillage was founded in 1995, thousands of women have come to the discussion groups on the Website to ask other women for help in paring down their expenses, and to celebrate their "frugal victories" as they discovered how to get more out of life for less. They've sought answers on cutting grocery bills, freeing themselves of debt, decorating their homes on a budget, and even (yes!) how to indulge themselves and their families without breaking the bank. In this book you'll find the very best solutions women have shared with each other in iVillage's online discussion groups.

iVillage would like to thank the members of ParentsPlace (www.parentsplace.com), Parent Soup (www.parentsoup.com), the Money Channel, and the Home & Garden Channel for sharing their words of wisdom and inspiration. Without them, this book would not exist. We'd also like to thank the hundreds of community leaders who host our online discussion and support groups for the care, concern, and support they provide to our visitors and members. And we'd like to thank Justin Schwartz, who provided invaluable assistance in helping us gather advice from the members of the iVillage community.

INTRODUCTION

◆

WHO IS THE FRUGAL WOMAN?

Frugal: adj. *Economical in use or expense; prudently saving or sparing; not wasteful.*

GIVEN THAT YOU'RE READING THIS PAGE, CHANCES ARE you've asked yourself at least once *Do I really need all this stuff? And why am I paying so much for it?* Maybe you're contemplating a credit card bill that outstrips your savings account by several digits. Or surveying a closet full of clothes worn once, and not worth the purchase. Or wondering why you just paid $7 for a sandwich that would cost you $1.50 to make at home. But could *you* really bring yourself to be *frugal?*

Isn't the Frugal Woman the old lady who reuses every tea bag five times? The one who "regifts" the junk from the back of her closet and wraps it in newspaper? The one who never spends a dime on anything fun or frivolous and alienates everyone she knows with her miserly ways?

News flash: Frugal Women across America are dressing their kids in brand-name clothes, getting their hair done in salons, buying antique furniture, eating gourmet meals, giving gifts that wow their friends and families—all while socking money away in their savings and retirement accounts, living free of credit card debt, and feeling secure about tomorrow while enjoying today.

On iVillage, thousands of women gather every month to trade tips about living well on less. They celebrate frugal victories and support each other as they look to redefine their lifestyles. They've embraced frugality for many reasons—but the end result for all is that they enjoy their lives more. Here's what some of them have to say:

"I still buy what I want now—I just do it differently. I replaced the malls with yard sales and consignment shops. I started cooking at home. Eating out is a special treat, not the source for everyday meals. Clipping coupons and watching for sales is fun now, almost like a hobby. It's a great way to challenge yourself. I've always heard that necessity is the mother of invention. Well, living frugally is the mother of creativity. You learn to use what you have, and you appreciate things more. I am always thinking of new ways to use what I already have. Sure, I still like to buy, but I don't go into debt to do it."

———— ✦ ————

"A friend and I recently decided that it's time to get a grip on our out-of-control spending habits. We've both gone on a 'no-spending-money' diet. For 30 days, we've decided not to spend money on anything that isn't a necessity. We're buying groceries and gas, paying bills, and that's it. No stops at the corner coffeehouse, no magazines in the grocery checkout, no drive-through burgers, no trips to the bookstore, mall, and so on. Three weeks into this, we're amazed at the amount of money we have left at the end of each pay period. That money is going to help us catch up on our bills. Our 'contract' is renewable at the end of 30 days, and I think we're both going to go for another month. By then we should be completely caught up, and we may have silenced the 'material girl' that lives inside us both. It wasn't nearly as hard as we'd anticipated. In fact, it's actually fun. We've gotten very creative when it comes to finding ways to get what we want. I'm making iced mochas at home, we're brown-bagging lunches, patronizing the public library instead of the bookstore, going for walks in the park instead of walking through the mall—lots of little changes, but they add up. The sense of regaining control has been a huge bonus."

Frugal Women come from all walks of life, and they have all sorts of reasons for embracing a sparer lifestyle. It's not just debt or excessive spending habits that motivate them. Sometimes frugality is as much about getting more value for the money you *do* spend as it is about spending less.

"I am a middle-class, fairly well-educated professional who happens to be frugal. I'm frugal because I do not like paying more than I have to for substandard-quality products simply because they are new or there is a great deal of advertising associated with the products. I seldom buy clothes at discount stores, not because I am a snob, but because I can find better quality in thrift stores and yard sales. If I am in a regular store it may well be a 'label store.' I am there for two reasons: I need to know what things cost so I know what a good deal is, and sometimes 'label' stores have unbelievable clearance sales. I pick the things that are important to me, and a frugal lifestyle allows me to attain the goals I set for myself."

———— ✦ ————

"I have always been frugal, though at some times more so than others. To me, being frugal means getting the most for your money. If I get something nice that I need or really want for a great price, then I feel good about myself. If I spend too much, I feel dumb. It's as simple as that. Being frugal isn't about being cheap, it's about using your money wisely."

Ever think about how much time you waste trying to find storage spaces for all the junk you don't need? Or how much garbage is created by the packaging of the (pricey) disposable things you buy over and over? How much gasoline you use taking three trips to the store because you didn't make a list the first time? Sure you have.

The Frugal Woman is not just interested in spending less. She wants the rewards that come with a more pared-down life: organized living and working spaces, more time spent with loved ones, leisure activities that engage the body and mind instead of the wallet, knowing that she's contributed to the well-being of the environment by reusing and recycling—and even a greater appreciation for the material items she does have. As one Frugal Woman writes,

"I want to free myself of certain beliefs about modern life: that we need certain labels, brands, cars, and so on, to make us happy. I want an organized home, but that's impossible as long as I have too much stuff. Consuming isn't good for me— or the environment. I want to be a better steward of the earth, pollute less, care more. I think when I get down to the nitty-gritty, I can have a clearer sense of what is important. I can have my luxuries, but understanding what is real luxury and what is excess, is becoming very important to me.

"I have four children, so certain 'simple' things are not going to happen right now—things like peace, quiet, and tidiness to the degree I would like. But if I can impart empathy and respect for their fellow humans to my children, I figure they will understand what is truly important in life. I want them to understand the need to do and be and find meaning, rather than to buy and accumulate. Pretty lofty, but there you go."

With this book, you'll learn the dollar-stretching secrets that have worked for thousands of women on iVillage. You'll find out how to make the best use of what you already have, identify what you really need in your life (and what you don't), find out how to get the necessities (and even a few luxuries) for less, and cut down on wasting resources (yours and the earth's). You'll see how to apply frugal principles to everything from grocery shopping to home decorating to holiday celebrations. Plus you'll hear from Frugal Women themselves about the "Rich Life Rewards" they've found in following a sparer lifestyle.

The Frugal Woman is not cheap; she's a cost-conscious, savvy consumer who avoids wasting her time, her money, and her energy on things she doesn't need. She's organized about her money management, spending, and household planning. She's in control of her life. That's something to be proud of.

You can be a Frugal Woman. There are no dues to pay, no forms to sign—just an embracing of the belief that you *can* live well on less. The Frugal Women of this book will show you how to do it.

CHAPTER 1

THE FRUGAL WOMAN Manages Her Money

My frugal ways only began after I hit rock bottom. I woke up one morning and looked at someone who had squandered her money on everything, and knew I was in big trouble. I needed to make some serious changes.

It has taken me a couple of years to perfect my strategy. If you think I am 'doing without,' then you are mistaken. I have the things I need and some of the things I want; this helps me to keep an eye on my larger goals. I also want to *stress that I live happily. No bill collectors calling. I love going to the bank—I get recognition there because I'm a good customer. They tell me about specials on CD rates and even ask me for advice on how to save.*

The old me was beaten down. Now, money is empowering in more ways than one. Money is not evil; poverty is evil. It can drive good people to steal, cheat, lie, and even worse. Money problems can break up marriages and families. They can cause good parents to lash out at children and the people around them. Money in the bank brings peaceful thinking (not to mention compounded interest). When my thoughts are peaceful, I feel like I can achieve just about anything.

—S.T.

◆

THE FIRST STEP IN BEING FRUGAL IS TO TAKE CONTROL of your money: Figure out where it's going, how to spend less, and how to save more. This chapter is by no means a comprehensive guide to financial matters (for books that cover debt and money management in depth, see The Frugal Woman's Best Financial Reads on the next page, a list of books most recommended by the Frugal Women on iVillage). But you will learn the basics of tracking your spending, creating and following a budget, and savings principles that will help get you on your way to a more secure future.

THE FRUGAL WOMAN'S BEST FINANCIAL READS

Think frugally: Check these books out of the library, or buy used on Amazon.com or half.com.

$ *Debt-Proof Living* by Mary Hunt (Broadman & Holman Publishers, 1999)
What Frugal Women say: "It's the most sensible, easy-to-follow financial guide out there."

$ *How to Get Out of Debt, Stay Out of Debt, and Live Prosperously* by Jerrold Mundis (Bantam Books, 1990)
What Frugal Women say: "Jerrold Mundis believes that life is for living–not just scrimping and saving every last penny. You do need to get out of debt and have savings for emergencies and retirement. But you can still enjoy life. The important thing is balance, and knowing your financial priorities."

$ *Get What You Want in Life with the Money You Already Have* by Carol Keefe (Little Brown & Co., 1995)
What Frugal Women say: "Carol Keefe encourages you to remember you are *not* your debt; it's only money. She also shows you how you can allocate small amounts of money to make them work for you. This is the book I pull off my shelf and go over every time I'm feeling down about my debt!"

$ *9 Steps to Financial Freedom* by Suze Orman (Crown Publishers, 1997)
What Frugal Women say: "Really good. The book talks about the emotional relationship with money, and money as a living, growing thing that needs to be nurtured and how to nurture it."

The Frugal Woman Knows . . .

WHERE HER MONEY GOES

Do you constantly ask yourself *Where did all my money go?* at the end of every month? Before you can even begin figuring out how to spend less money, you need to figure out exactly what you're spending it on.

One Frugal Woman advises, "The best way to save is to find your 'leak'—in other words, where the money is going. Track your expenses—*all* of your expenses—including the can of soda, gas for the car, clothes, food, and so on. You should probably track for at least a month. Once your expenses are on paper, it becomes more real to everyone in the family and helps you pinpoint your leak."

Frugal Women on iVillage use a variety of tools to track their spending—some opt for computer programs such as Quicken or Microsoft Money; others find that a plain paper version (like the Spending Chart on page 5) works just as well. However you choose to track your spending, be detailed—and honest—about your habits. There's an old saying that we don't trip on mountains, we stumble on pebbles. And for many, it's the "pebbles" that trip up our budgets.

SPENDING CHART

Track your spending using this chart. For each day of the week, enter the amount you spend in each category. Use the blank spaces in each major category to add categories that fit your life. Enter all expenditures–whether you pay by cash, check, debit, or credit–as you make them. It helps to keep all your receipts and fill out the day's spending every night, so that no expenditures "slip" your mind. (If you don't make any expenditures in a given category during the week, leave those spaces blank.) Try to track your spending for at least a month to give yourself an idea of your overall monthly expenditures, so that you can better budget.

Week of _____

AMOUNT SPENT	Mon.	Tues.	Wed.	Thurs.	Fri.	Sat.	Sun.
Home							
Maintenance/Repairs							
Decorating							
Auto							
Repairs							
Gasoline							
Supplies (Wiper Fluid, etc.)							
Car Washes							
Clothing, Shoes, and Accessories							
Mine							
Spouse's							
Children's							
Laundry/Dry Cleaning/Tailor							

AMOUNT SPENT	Mon.	Tues.	Wed.	Thurs.	Fri.	Sat.	Sun.
Health and Beauty							
Medication							
Cosmetics							
Personal Care Items							
Food and Beverages							
Groceries							
Take Out/Delivery							
Restaurant Meals							
Snacks/Miscellaneous							
Entertainment							
Movies and Videos							
Books and Music							
Magazines and Newspapers							
Gifts							
Child Care							
Pet Care							
Charitable Donations							
Commuting							
Services and Utilities							
Electric							
Gas							
Water							
Cable TV							
Internet Access							
Phone (Landline and Cell)							

AMOUNT SPENT	Mon.	Tues.	Wed.	Thurs.	Fri.	Sat.	Sun.
Payments							
Rent/Mortgage							
Auto Loan/Lease							
Loans							
Credit Card							
Gym/Club Membership							
Organization Dues							

The Frugal Woman Knows...

DEBT IS A FOUR-LETTER WORD

The Frugal Woman despises debt, especially credit card debt. Simply put, there's nothing less frugal than having to pay extra for what you've already bought—that interest that compounds and piles up on top of the expenditures you've already made. Frugal Women overwhelmingly embrace a debt-free life—using frugal methods to get out of debt if they are in it, and to stay out of it once it's gone. (Realize, of course, even Frugal Women seldom try to buy a house without taking out a mortgage—although they watch mortgage rates and refinance as rates become more favorable.)

One of the simplest ways to stay free of debt, as one Frugal Woman comments, is to "live below your means. Even if you and your spouse/partner gross six figures, that doesn't necessarily mean that you can buy that Lexus, take that cruise, go skiing every winter; you don't really 'deserve' these things just because you make good salaries. Along the same lines, don't try to keep up with the Joneses; chances are, the Joneses are up to their eyeballs in debt and can't sleep at night."

One of the most common—and most important—recommendations made by Frugal Women on iVillage is to pay off any credit card debt you are carrying, and not to incur any further debt. "If you can't afford to pay for something with cash, check, or debit card," says one Frugal Woman, "you can't afford it."

The Frugal Woman Knows...
HOW TO CONTROL HER CREDIT CARDS

Some Frugal Women choose to live without credit cards altogether (often after having gotten out of massive debt from them). But that may not be practical or desirable for you. If you are carrying large balances from month to month, many would advise you to strongly consider taking a sharp pair of scissors to your cards. If you're not at the point of needing to cut up your plastic, try these methods to set limits for yourself.

Leave yourself reminders about their use.
"Tape a note on your credit cards with a saying like 'Emergencies Only' or something that makes you think twice before making a purchase."

Put them in safe hands (other than yours!).
"Give your credit cards to someone you trust (like your mom). You should be free to get them when you need them, but you have to tell the person what you're buying. This works because if you feel silly about explaining the item, you'll think twice about why you wanted it in the first place."

Set a monthly budget for their use, and pay in full every month.

"I never, ever leave a balance on my credit card. We don't buy it if we can't pay it in full at the end of the month. I refuse to pay finance charges for anything. I am a total tightwad!"

The Frugal Woman Knows . . .

THE DIFFERENCE BETWEEN A "NEED" AND A "WANT"

It's not wrong—or even "unfrugal"—to have "wants." But when you're making a budget, it's good to categorize what you absolutely need versus what you just want. Training yourself to question the necessity of any purchase (*before* you make it, not after) will help you get and stay on track with your spending. Identifying certain things as a "need" or a "want" is easy: A roof over your head is a need; the grande mocha cappuccino at the coffee emporium is a want. But even within categories that seem basic, choices exist. Here's how some Frugal Women have tackled the question of needs versus wants.

Redefine what qualifies as a basic.

"There are basics that we all need, such as shelter, clothes, food, and so on. But sometimes I have to look at the choices in the categories, such as shelter: Our house is about 1,800 square feet, but we moved here from a smaller two-bedroom apartment. The apartment was shelter, so did we 'need' a house? (Although some days, the house isn't big enough for all of us!) Same with clothes—I need shorts in the summer, but do I *need* big brand names, or do I just *want* them?"

If you already have several, another is a want.

"At this point, I believe that most clothes I buy for myself are wants. I have about 20 pairs of shoes; another pair can't possibly be a need! Clothes for the kids, on the other hand, are needs because they grow out of their clothes and can't wear them anymore."

If it's still usable, a new one is not a need.

"Most household items are wants, unless something I use regularly breaks. For example, I make waffles a lot with my waffle iron; if it breaks, I'll replace it and consider it a need. However, it's getting kind of old and grungy but it still works; if I decide I want a nice, new, pretty one, that would be a want. I just make sure I leave plenty of room in my budget for wants because it's the wants that can make life enjoyable and fun."

Saving is always a need.

"Retirement savings are at the top of our budget, and that money gets saved no matter what. We also have savings for emergencies."

There are no absolute answers to what's a need or a want for you—but as you work toward creating a budget you can live with day-in-and-day-out (or are in a situation that requires you to drastically cut down on your spending), take a hard look at all your expenditures and determine what's essential. For instance, your clothes need drying after washing. But hanging them to dry instead of using the dryer accomplishes the same thing, and for free. It's essential that you (or your spouse) get to work. But carpooling, taking mass transportation, or walking may get you there just as well. The bottom line: If you can do without it, or do with less of it, it's a want. (For more ways on paring down, see S.T.'s Spend-Less, Save-More Strategies on page 17.)

The Frugal Woman Knows...
HOW TO BUILD AND FOLLOW A BUDGET

The premise behind formulating a budget is simple: Figure out how much money you have coming in and how much money *must* go out each month, and then align your expenditures so that the latter does not exceed the former. For many, though, it's not so easy. Following are the top recommendations from the Frugal Women of iVillage on how to begin this exercise. You may find the Cash Flow Calculator on page 14 helpful in working through your budget, line-by-line.

1. Pay yourself first: Set aside a percentage of your paycheck (many recommend 10 to 20 percent) to go directly into savings and retirement accounts.

2. Calculate your regular fixed expenses, such as rent or mortgage, utilities, food, child care, and so on. (Gathering several months of past bills and receipts can help accurately account for all your expenditures.) Don't forget to include such periodic expenses as property taxes and car insurance.

3. Put money toward paying off credit card debt or loans.

4. Allow for weekly spending cash for yourself and your spouse. Most likely, this will entail setting priorities: the magazine at the newsstand *or* the coffee at Starbucks; the new pair of shoes *or* the haircut at the salon.

Once you've created a budget on paper, the real challenge becomes living within it. Here are some clever methods Frugal Women use to stay on track with their spending.

Make your budget conform to your life.

"Make categories that apply to your own situation. For instance, I always worry about how much we spend on pet supplies, so I have a pets category. My husband thinks I spend too much on crafting so we have a craft category. If you are using a software program to track your spending, use the categories that come with it as a guideline, but add what you need."

Track expenditures as they arise.

"Carry a notebook with you and write down your purchases as you make them, just like you would with your checkbook. For instance, I drove through McDonald's this morning for a drink, and as I was waiting in line I pulled out my notebook and recorded the cost. Makes it much easier than trying to remember!"

Separate cash allocated for specific purposes.

"Writing out my weekly budget just doesn't work for me. I finally started taking the budgeted money out of the bank, and putting the cash in separate, marked envelopes—gas, groceries, and so on. For instance, if I have $20 budgeted for lunches one week, and can use only what's in my 'lunch money' envelope, I'm a lot less likely to blow $10 on Monday and leave myself short for the next four days."

Use refillable gift/debit cards.

"For monthly budgeting, try using the refillable gift or debit cards. You can get them at most retailers nowadays. For instance, say your grocery budget is $300 a month. On the first of the month, fill up your gift card to that amount. If it looks like you're about to run short, you can modify your eating habits to make the most of the last of your money. If you have extra money on the card at the end of the month, you can either put it toward the next month or bank it! For people like me who have tried the cash in the envelope system and had it fail because having cash around was too tempting, it may be an easier way to keep your budget in order."

Break your money into separate accounts.

"I have separate accounts for different purposes. One savings account is for the monthly total I have for food, gas, and so on. Then I move the weekly amount for that spending into one checking/debit account. I have a second savings account in which I put the money I set aside for bills, and use a separate checking account only for writing checks for those bills. I also have a CD as my 'emergency fund.' I bank online so it's very easy to keep it straight with MS Money."

CASH FLOW CALCULATOR

Try using the Cash Flow Calculator to see how your expenses compare to your income. If you've been recording your expenditures using the Spending Chart on page 5 or by another method, filling the expense section of the Cash Flow Calculator should be easy. If you haven't, go through several months' worth of receipts to make the best estimate on spending you can (and start tracking your spending now!).

1. Figure your monthly income.

Salary (after taxes)	$ _____
Other Pay (such as bonuses; divide annual amount by 12)	$ _____
Investment Income	$ _____
Scholarships	$ _____
Money from Other Sources	$ _____
Line 1: TOTAL INCOME	$ _____

2. Tally your monthly expenses.

Rent or Mortgage	$ _____
Gas and Electric	$ _____
Telephone	$ _____
Groceries	$ _____
Eating Out (including coffee and drinks!)	$ _____
Car Payments	$ _____
Commuting/Transit	$ _____
Loan Payments	$ _____
Health Insurance	$ _____
Other Insurance	$ _____

Home Maintenance	$ _____
Laundry/Dry Cleaning	$ _____
Child Care	$ _____
Cable TV	$ _____
Internet Access	$ _____
Books, Music	$ _____
Movies	$ _____
Other Entertainment	$ _____
Clothes	$ _____
Vacation (divide annual costs by 12)	$ _____
Gifts	$ _____
Newspapers and Magazines	$ _____
Pet Care	$ _____
Gym	$ _____
Other Memberships	$ _____
Religious, Charitable Donations	$ _____
Miscellaneous	$ _____
Line 2: TOTAL EXPENSES	$ _____

3. Calculate your cash flow.

Deduct the sum on Line 2 from the sum on Line 1 (Line 1 − Line 2 = Cash flow). If you get a negative number, that means your expenses outstrip your income, and it's time to reduce spending where you can. Take a look at each line item above, and determine which ones you can cut back on.

If you get a positive number–good for you! You may still want to look at where you can reduce your spending, and increase your savings, but you're on the right track.

The Frugal Woman Knows . . .

MONEY IN THE BANK FEELS GOOD

Frugal Women employ a multitude of savvy savings strategies that help them build their bank accounts slowly but steadily. Their methods follow one overarching principle: Put away a little bit regularly rather than waiting to put a large amount in your account occasionally. Then, just watch your savings grow!

Save a dollar a day.

"Try to put a little money away every day during the month—$1, $2, $5, whatever you can afford. At the end of the month, deposit the money in your savings account. Think about it—everybody can take that $1 or $2 they would normally spend on coffee or candy or other junk food and put that in an envelope. Or just look in your wallet at the end of the day, and take the money from what you have left. Even though it's a small amount, it adds up quickly. In just a few months I've saved nearly $200, and it's in a savings account earning interest. Like I said, it's a little at a time, but it does add up. It's easy and painless."

Start a change jar.

"I used to be so annoyed by the change at the bottom of my bag, or the change my husband left lying around the house. When I was pregnant, I put some jars in the baby's room, and every time I found some coins, I put them in a jar. By the time my daughter was born, I had over $120 in those jars! So, I opened a savings account and bought a savings bond. Now, at the end of every month, I buy a $25 savings bond for my daughter. All of my friends and family are now doing it too."

"Hide" money from yourself.

"My husband and I were getting off track with our saving, so we tried some new tricks. I have been sending all my paychecks to another bank account, which is in another state. I have access to the money if there is an emergency, but since the money isn't in my household checking account, I don't think about having it. In a way, I am 'hiding' the money from myself. So far, we have put away about $1,100."

S.T.'s Spend-Less, Save-More Strategies

The Frugal Woman from the beginning of this chapter, who shared her story of hitting rock bottom finan-cially and recovering, devised many ways to conserve cash and then sock it away in savings. Her fru-gality took her from deep in debt to financial security—and her advice can help you too.

SPENDING LESS

Use public transportation.

I take advantage of public transportation. Sure, it takes longer to get to and from work, and sometimes I watch with envy as others speed past me in their cars while I stand out in the cold, waiting for the subway or the bus. But I am saving about $125 a month on parking. Not only do I save money by using less gas, I also help to save the environment.

Breakfast at home.

In the mornings, I make my breakfast at home. Buying expensive foods like muffins, bagels, juice, and coffee on the way to work can really add up.

Carry a lunch.

I make my lunch at home and bring it to work. I do treat myself to a lunch out occasionally—it's more enjoy-able now because I know my bills are paid.

Bring in snacks.

Rather than frequenting those expensive vending machines, I keep a snack drawer at work, with goodies I made at home or bought on sale.

Plan for treats.

I treat myself to special dinners on the weekends, because I always watch for specials at the supermarket, keep a price book, and shop with coupons.

Shop "used."

I found a couple of friendly consignment shops.

Control cell phone use.

I have a cell phone, but since I only use it for emergencies, my bill is the same every month.

Out with the old!

If I want to buy something new, I hold a small garage sale first to get rid of things I no longer use. Most recently, I wanted to buy a beautiful new dressing table. I put my old dressing table up for sale, along with other unused items I pulled out of closets and drawers. Anything that I hadn't used for a year or more, I offered for sale.

Watch cleaning costs.

I avoid labels that say *dry clean only.* When something does need to be dry cleaned, I use Dryel to keep my clothes fresh.

Try updating things.

I look at my furnishings carefully before I think of throwing them out, to see if I can update them. Sometimes all it takes is a new coat of paint, or some new handles. Clothes dye is great for making over your bedsheets.

SAVING MORE

Pay yourself first.

I get paid every two weeks, and before any checks are written, I pay myself. I deposit into my savings account for my "old age" fund, my condo fund, my "freedom" account that I use for emergencies (flat tires, veterinarian bills), and my contingency fund (at least three months of salary).

Take advantage of employer matching.

I always contribute to my 401(k) because my employer matches it. There is no better way to save for retirement.

Watch interest amounts.

I closely monitor my savings accounts; when they reach a certain level, I sign up for a higher-yield account.

Avoid monthly fees.

I maintain a high enough balance in my bank accounts so that my bank doesn't charge me monthly usage fees. I get free checks, free traveler's checks, and interest on my checking account, as well as higher interest on my savings and CD accounts.

Save that spare change.

I never spend my spare change. I drop my change in my piggy bank every night and deposit it frequently so I won't be tempted to spend it.

"Splurge" on savings and donations.

I have money earmarked for my church and a charity. When I get a raise, I increase spending in only two areas: my savings and my charitable contributions.

Save those bonuses.

When I receive the occasional bonus, small tax return, or gifts of money on holidays, I keep 20 percent for myself to splurge and then divide the rest among my savings accounts.

RICH LIFE REWARDS:
A FRUGAL WOMAN'S TALE

Before I married my current husband, I was always very cognizant of money and the value of paying yourself first. I compiled a significant portfolio. So, why did I have such a large credit card balance? I felt so ashamed when I revealed $17,000 worth of credit card debt before our marriage. My husband is truly frugal. I have learned so much from him about day-to-day spending and he has learned about long-term investments from me. We are the perfect complement to each other.

Before we were even married, we formed a trust to protect our finances in the future and to prepare for the ends of our lives. Today we each have one credit card (at one time I had six) and the balance is paid every month. We use a debit card that automatically deducts purchases from our checking account. We dealt with my credit card insanity by using a home equity loan to pay it off. At least we could deduct the interest for that.

Ken loves to visit yard and estate sales. The man has a gift! He found my wedding present, a walnut Chickering baby grand piano at a yard sale for $1,400! *[Editor's note: These antique pianos typically go for about $25,000.]* One day he came home with an unopened box of Chanel #5 cologne and perfume. He had paid $5! Since our wedding I have ventured into new hobbies, such as stamping and quilting, along with my old favorites: counted cross-stitch, embroidery, and crocheting. Trust me, I have yet to store-buy any yarn, embroidery floss, stamps, ink, and fabric. Ken finds all that I could possibly need at yard sales. When my first husband died, I was left with lots of beautiful things and money. Over the 10 years that I was a widow, I would have cheerfully cashed in everything for one more hour of his time. I learned the greatest lesson in life: There is an enormous difference between want and need.

Now, Ken and I have all that we need! We need each other. We enjoy our time together and spend our time and assets as best we can. I am truly happy.

—Claudia Tibbetts, Lansdale, Pennsylvania

◆

CHAPTER 2

THE FRUGAL WOMAN
Goes Shopping

To me, being frugal is not about being cheap; it is about not paying full price if I don't have to. It is such a great reward to find a bargain. When shopping—be it for groceries or furniture—I always comparison shop before I buy, because I then know that I got the best deal out there. We do not have to live frugally. We choose to, however, because then we have more time and more money to spend on the things that mean the most to us—like family time.

Being frugal at the grocery store allows us to go out to weekly dinners, being frugal when buying clothes allows us to buy more from the same money. There are many rewards from being frugal but to me the biggest is being able to give my children the things they need and want (though they are not spoiled) without paying an arm and a leg for them.

—Cathy Barnt, Glendale, Arizona

◆

SHOPPING—WITH ITS EXPENDITURE OF MONEY—COULD be perceived as the Frugal Woman's greatest nemesis. And, perhaps, shopping needlessly and thoughtlessly is. But the Frugal Woman knows that shopping is also one of the greatest adventures and is truly a test of her ability to stretch a dollar and get the most for her money.

As Frugal Women will tell you, there's an art to smart shopping. It goes beyond sticking to sales and using coupons (which we'll cover shortly). Being a smart shopper means knowing what an item is worth, and where to get the best price on it. It's about finding new venues to get the stuff you love, and knowing how to work a sale.

The Frugal Woman Knows...

KEEPING A LEVEL HEAD IN THE STORE
KEEPS MONEY IN YOUR POCKET

There you are, innocently strolling through the store aisles, perhaps on an errand with a friend, or with one specific, budgeted purchase to make. And then it jumps out at you: that thing that you have to have. It's so cute. It's not much. It's . . . an impulse buy.

Seven ways Frugal Women beat the urge to impulse buy:

1. Think before you buy.

"I ask myself before each expenditure if it is for something I *really* need, or if it's something I just kind of want, or if it's comfort buying. Comfort buying is just like comfort eating, except instead of getting fat you end up broke with a very cluttered house. I try to make a wish list and a need list and keep them separate from each other. Unless it's food or a basic household item (like soap or cleansers), I wait for a week before purchasing. One of the tricks marketers use to convince us to buy stuff we don't really need is to convince us that it won't be there in a week, or that it will be more expensive if we don't buy right now. The truth is, it's really expensive to impulse buy instead of waiting and keeping a level head."

2. Analyze what you'll really get out of it.

"I tell myself that if our ancestors could live simply, so can we. Most of our 'needs' are market-driven anyway. Do you really need every sweater in every color? When shopping, I ask myself *Do I really need this item, or do I have something at home that can perform the same service?* and *Is the price equal to the enjoyment factor?*"

3. Carry cash, not credit.

"If you leave your plastic at home, you will be less apt to part with your cash and make impulse purchases."

4. Don't bring money to spare.

"To avoid compulsive spending, just leave your money at home. If you are going somewhere, know what you are after. Take enough cash to get only what you're going for, and leave the rest of the cash, checks, and credit cards at home. Works like a charm for us."

5. Realize it's not a bargain if you don't need it.

"Resist the temptation of buying something *just* because it's on sale. Maybe it feels good to say 'Hey, look at this great deal I got.' But it feels a lot worse when you realize later on that you don't really like it or need it."

6. Play the waiting game.

"If I really, really want something, then I'll get it. However, usually I try to make myself wait for a couple of weeks to see if I still want it. It's funny how our material desires come and go in our consumer culture. Something that is appealing one week is not so much so the next week. However, if I find week after week I am wishing for something—a rubber spatula, a pair of black pants, new running shoes—I will start shopping around."

7. Don't buy things you don't have room for.

"One thing that helps me avoid impulse shopping is my dislike for clutter. I used to be a spendthrift, but when I started living a more simple life, I went through a de-cluttering phase. I totally cleaned house and hauled tons of stuff to Goodwill.

What a feeling! I felt so freed. Owning stuff, especially stuff you don't need or use, can be a burden. Now, when I shop I always evaluate my purchases in terms of clutter potential. This helps me to avoid purchasing trendy clothing, or something that is just 'too good' of a deal to pass up. Now I keep it simple."

The Frugal Woman Knows . . .
COMPARISON IS HER SECRET WEAPON

Seek and ye shall find . . . a better price. So thinks the Frugal Woman. Nothing quite compares to the thrill of getting exactly what you want for the very least you have to pay for it. But that requires a little investigative research before handing over your money to any retailer. Whether it's a new sofa or your monthly beauty aids, knowing who has the best price can help you spot a bargain in an instant. Here are three tips for finding the best price on *anything*.

Create a price book.

"A price book is a great tool for saving! Here's what I did: I collected the sales fliers for two weeks from all the area stores. I also threw my store receipts in a basket. Then I sat down one night with loose-leaf paper, a three-ring binder, and a calculator. I only wrote down products and brands I would buy. Some tips for organizing your price book:

$ Each page should be for just one item, like toothpaste. Then, for instance, you might list Colgate, Crest, and one or two store brands.

$ For each brand, write down the store, the weight/size, and the price. Make sure you figure out cost per unit. [*Editor's note: Stores typically list this on the shelf tag, next to the actual price of the product.*] You may assume that certain packages are the same size or weight, but they aren't when you look closely. It does take some time, but it's well worth it.

$ Use sheets of paper so you can move them around to alphabetize.

Remember to take your price book with you on shopping trips, so you can refer to it while making your selections at the store."

Take your hunt online.

"We saved a lot by buying a couch online. We shopped around at local stores, and once we knew what manufacturer and fabric we wanted, we ordered from a store a few states away. Even including the delivery charges, we saved $300 over the best price we could get locally."

See if your store will match another's advertised sale prices.

"Look through the sale ads for your area (Target, pharmacy, grocery store, any place) and find what you need. Then make a notation on your grocery list with the store name and the sale price that you want to match. Your store location may need to see the ads, so take them with you. Circle or highlight the items in the ads so they can be easily found—for instance, put a note on front of your sales circulars with a list of the items you are going to price-match. If they don't want to see the ad, they may want to know the store name. Much will depend on your particular store's procedures. To make it easy at check-out time, when I get to the cashier lane, I put all the stuff I want to price-match at the very end and I tell the cashier that I'm going to price-match everything from such-and-such item on back. When we get to the price-matching stuff I tell her what the price is and she keys it into the computer system. It's that easy!"

SETTING UP A PRICE BOOK ON YOUR COMPUTER

If you have a computer, you can use a spreadsheet program such as Excel to help you create your price book. Here's one Frugal Woman's method:

$ First create a worksheet with a column on the left side listing all of the products that you buy or might buy. Group similar items together, like health and beauty aids. (A big advantage of using your computer is that you can add extra spaces anytime, if you think of other products you'd like to add to the list.)

$ Next, in the top row put the name of each store you are comparing (Wal-Mart, Target, pharmacies, local supermarkets, and so on).

$ Now print out your price sheet and take a copy with you whenever you go shopping.

For example, your price book for health and beauty aids might be set up like this:

Product	Product Size	Price at Wal-Mart	Price at Target	Price at CVS	Price at Supermarket
Crest Regular Anti-Cavity Formula	8.2 oz.				
Colgate Total Plus Whitening Paste	7.8 oz.				
Pert Plus—Extra Conditioner	13.5 oz.				
Finesse Enhancing Formula Shampoo & Conditioner	15 oz.				
Jergen's Skin Care Skin Soothing Lotion	10 oz.				
Vaseline Aloe & Naturals Formula Lotion	11 oz.				

The Frugal Woman Knows . . .

TO BREAK HERSELF OF THE

BIG-NAME STORE HABIT

Amazing as it seems, you can get the best in brand names—even designer labels—without ever setting foot in a "full price" department store. Shopping at factory and designer outlets is one well-known venue for savings, of course (check out Outletbound.com at www.outletbound.com to find outlet centers near you, or go to RealOutlets.com at www.realoutlets.com for online "outlet" shopping).

But there are a host of other sources favored by discriminating Frugal Women—here are places to find some of the best deals on brand-name merchandise.

Overstock Stores and Websites

"If you're on a tight budget, but prefer not to buy used or second-hand merchandise, search the Web for sites that specialize in selling 'overstock merchandise' at liquidation prices. Everything is brand-new, not refurbished. They buy excess merchandise from major retailers and manufacturers, and you can get expensive items way below retail. Some online retailers even offer warranties."

Yard Sales, Garage Sales, and Flea Markets

"Try checking out garage sales in the more affluent neighborhoods—they can be a great place to buy clothes. I've purchased things with the price tags still attached!"

Thrift Stores

"I find great buys on name-brand clothes at the local thrift stores. I've bought entire outfits for $8, and jackets for less than $5. The brands range from Eddie Bauer to Liz Claiborne. People don't believe me when I tell them what I spent. Almost all my boys' clothes have come from thrift shops, too—brand-new jeans for 75 cents! How can you beat that? The only drawback is that you can't always find exactly what you're looking for, but the thrill of finding such a great bargain makes up for it."

Discount Chains

"I like bargain stores like TJ Maxx, though sometimes it takes a bit more effort to find something great. My best trick is to look in every size and every section, even the men's section. Whoever marks the merchandise is often unfamiliar with European sizing and labels, so items are not always categorized correctly. For example, I found a pair of new Bally loafers for just $6. The box said size six, but the imported shoe fit my size nine feet just fine. Also, ask the staff when new merchandise is put on the sales floor. Avoid the weekend crowds at all costs. Midweek evenings generally yield the best finds."

The Frugal Woman Knows...

HOW TO BE A GARAGE SALE PRO

In addition to the sheer delight of enjoying a spring day in the company of a good friend or close family member, "garage sale-ing" can yield incredible bargains. But there's an art to it, as one Frugal Woman explains. Here are her top five tips.

1. If you are looking for a particular item, think of the neighborhood you're most likely to find it in. For example, for small cheap kitchen items, look for garage sales in areas where people are more transient, such as apartment areas. You're not going to find expensive furniture in apartment neighborhoods.

2. Know what it's worth. Note the prices. You shouldn't pay more than 10 percent of the retail price. If the prices are off on a few items you are familiar with, move on. However, highly desirable stuff such as antique furniture or bicycles usually sells for a higher percentage.

3. Buy from the right seller. Don't buy from "semi-pros"—you'll know them because they plaster the neighborhood with their signs. They'll have multiple items such as three or four vacuum cleaners. They'll be on main streets. They know what it's worth and you won't get a deal from them. Avoid sales advertised in newspapers—the hawks will be there early and they'll clean out the deals quickly. Look for amateurs on back streets.

4. Shop the right time of the year. Right before the school year starts, and right after it ends, are good times because the weather is nice, and a lot of people are moving and they are more willing to abandon better stuff.

5. Haggle on the price, but be nice. *Really* nice! You want the seller to be your friend. Find an item at a good price and then offer between half and a third less, then dicker to the price you'll accept. You can use poverty or damage as dicker points. Smile while you negotiate! If you offer less than a third of what they're asking, you will anger the seller. Walk away from the deal after you've dickered to let the buyer offer one more discount. (The exception to this rule is if another hawk is lurking.) And don't get into a bidding war with another customer. Let them win.

The Frugal Woman Knows...

HOW TO SHOP AT THE FLEA MARKET

Part of the fun of flea market shopping is finding the unexpected. However, as one Frugal Woman experienced in the world of flea markets says, "A day at a flea market can result in visual overkill. You won't be able to pick out special pieces after a while." To help you keep a clear head and get maximum enjoyment (and bargains), here are some of her guidelines.

$ Go searching for one thing, maybe a nice cup and saucer or a mirror. You will notice other things, and it's okay to buy them, but it's easier to find what you're looking for if you focus on just the cups and saucers, or the mirrors.

$ Don't rush. Dealers are always putting more stuff out as other pieces sell, so you will never see everything. Count on luck and your expertise to help you find a treasure.

$ Dress for the occasion in old jeans and a plain top with ratty sneakers—no designer labels or trendy clothes.

$ Carry small bills in small numbers in different pockets—never pull out a wad of cash to pay after a bargaining session. Don't carry a purse—it will get in your way and in the excitement of the moment you might lose it.

$ Take each purchase back to the car instead of carrying it all over. At large flea markets it pays to bring along a helper (child, grandchild, husband).

$ If you are out of town and flying home, instead of carrying your purchase on the plane, wrap it up and take it to the local UPS Store or post office to be shipped home.

For a Rich Life . . .

START YOUR OWN BUYING CLUB OR CO-OP

Buying clubs and co-ops allow a group of individuals or families to take advantage of bulk discounts by pooling their funds and then divvying up the products. Here's how one Frugal Woman used this strategy to ensure she could get her family the organic items she valued.

I worked at a natural foods store for over four years, and was very spoiled. When I left to have a baby, I knew I couldn't go back. But how was I going to continue to get organic foods and natural health and beauty aids for my family at a discounted price?

Well, I started a buying club/co-op. There are just four of us. Two run a food/grocery co-op every two months through a supportive local natural foods store. One runs a weekly organic produce co-op off her porch. I run a monthly buying club for herbs, spices, and health and beauty aids.

It works great! You have to get used to spending money in big lumps for quantity, but it can be done. I have cut my weekly spending by half. I feel good that I can still offer my family the quality we are used to, without compromising our budget.

The Frugal Woman Knows . . .

SIMPLICITY AND QUALITY SAVE MONEY

One part of saving money is to spend less on any given item. The other side of the coin is to buy fewer items, less frequently. How do you do that with high-use items such as clothes and shoes? Here's what some Frugal Women have to say.

Look for what will last.

"When I shop for clothes, durability is a must. I tend to buy most of my clothes in neutral colors, and then add fun (and affordable) accessories that are in vogue."

Don't buy into trends.

"I pay a little more for high-quality clothes, accessories, and housewares. And I stick with classic, less-trendy styles. A bargain isn't always a bargain if it doesn't last. I expect my things to be durable enough to last several years, and to still be in style."

Shop for deals in brand names.

"Here is a way to save when it's back-to-school time: Try the designer discount store for kid's shoes—if you buy good ones they will last longer. There is a good chance you'll find good deals on the name-brand sneakers that your kids like."

The Frugal Woman Knows . . .
WHEN SHE BUYS IS AS IMPORTANT AS WHERE SHE BUYS

Here's how to finesse your sales-scooping timing.

Be first in line for markdowns.

"I figured out that Gap stores in my area marked down their merchandise on Tuesday nights. So I get there at opening time on Wednesday morning to get the best deals."

Go just before closing time.

"Try to hit flea markets or garage sales at the end of the day, when everyone is about to start packing. They're more likely to give you a great deal to avoid having to cart it back themselves, or take it back in the house."

Hit post-season sales.

"I buy holiday cards *after* Christmas. I also buy clothing after the retail season ends, so I get my fall and winter clothes in January and February, and spring and summer clothes in August."

Use layaway, and watch for a sale.

"At most major discount stores, if you have an item on layaway, and then the item goes on sale, they will often automatically give you the lowest price. To be sure, take your layaway slip to the counter, and ask them to give you the sale price. It's a good way to reserve those hard-to-find items, spread the expense out over time, and still take advantage of those sales closer to the holidays."

The Frugal Woman Knows...

HOW TO DRESS HER KIDS IN STYLE (WITHOUT BREAKING THE BANK)

You love watching your kids grow—except when you see them growing out of their clothes. Here's how Frugal Women keep their kids smartly outfitted, smartly.

Buy off-season.

"I buy clothes for my kids for next year off the clearance rack this year. For example, at the end of winter, I take advantage of the sales and buy winter clothes for next year's winter. I rarely need to buy anything new when the next winter comes around. I try to hit Old Navy and Gap at least once a month to check out the clearance racks. If it's not on sale, I don't buy it."

Make friends with the salespeople.

"Many major department stores pay their salespeople either completely or partially on commission. I have a salesperson at every major department store in my area. When I go in and see the most adorable Tommy Hilfiger shorts for full price, I let the salesperson know that I am interested. She keeps me posted—yes, she'll call to let me know when items I like go on sale."

Buy classic and big.

"Polo shirts, chinos, khakis, and jeans never go out of style. Have you ever noticed how the size you want is *never* on sale for $3.99? Even if you don't need clothes at the moment, buying classic allows you to buy larger sizes when they are on sale, and eventually kids will grow into them. Take advantage of the sale prices, and put the clothes away in the closet for a few months."

Avoid the back-to-school rush.

"Try to spread school purchases out over the year. Try, for instance, to get beyond the idea that underwear and socks have to replaced every September. If everyone's things are still decent and wearable, I hold off until later in the school year."

Buy the best you can afford.

"A good quality book bag is a better buy in the long run than a cheap one. My kids have used theirs for as long as three years. I wash them occasionally in cold water on the delicate cycle."

FASHION DOESN'T HAVE TO COST A FORTUNE

$ For beauty bargains and other indulgences, watch the Freebies & Deals page on Substance.com (an iVillage site).

$ If you live in the New York or Los Angeles metro areas, check out dailycandy.com. Its daily emails regularly highlight upcoming sample sales, at which you can scoop up name-brand buys at huge discounts off regular retail.

$ Check out RealOutlets.com for online sales (up to 60 percent off!) from such brands as Eddie Bauer, J.Crew, Spiegel, Mikasa, and more.

$ Get on the mailing lists (both email and regular mail) of your favorite department and specialty stores, to find out when they are running their seasonal sales. Discounts can run as high as 50 percent off everything from designer clothes to housewares, and those on the stores' mailing lists often receive notice or extra-savings promotions to use during the sales.

$ Many cities and metropolitan areas have local weekly or monthly magazines highlighting everything from regional events to local personalities. Often these publications feature a column with updates on better-quality stores running seasonal clearance sales, special shopping events, and other savings opportunities.

$ Check out Citysearch.com for listings of outlet stores and sample sales in your area.

The Frugal Woman Knows...

THERE'S MORE TO NAVIGATING THE GROCERY STORE THAN FINDING THE DAIRY AISLE

Feeding your family can take up the bulk of your income. But it doesn't have to. Here are some tricks Frugal Women use to stick to their food budgets without living on plain water and raw greens. (For more advice on managing the frugal kitchen, see Chapter 3.)

Stock up on store brands.

"Coupons are good, but you're forced to buy the expensive name-brand products. Try store brands for big savings. Some items—food, paper products, cleaning supplies—are cheaper than national brands even with a coupon. You'll have to test them out for yourself, but I've had great luck with my local store brands."

Don't buy what you won't use.

"If you have a small family, over-shopping can be your worst enemy. It might be better to shop a couple of times a week for only the items you need. Never buy more than a few days' worth of produce unless it's something you can freeze."

Shop online.

"If you like a particular item and buy a lot of it, search the Internet to see if you can get a better price by ordering online. I've found that it is generally less expensive for me to have certain products delivered than to buy them at the grocery store."

Learn to love loss leaders.

"Shop for loss leaders—most grocery stores advertise a few products each week at a great deal. These are called 'loss leaders' because the stores often sell them at or below cost. The point in offering these deals is to entice you to shop there. Keep an eye on the ads for great deals, but don't be charmed into buying things that are not a good deal just because you are there."

Go it alone.

"Leave your husband at home. Every time mine comes, things just fall off the shelf and into the cart!"

Make a list, and check it twice.

"Keep a list of items you've run out of on the fridge. Go through the store ads before you shop so that you can see which store is offering the best deal. Take your list with you to the supermarket so you don't get sidetracked."

Have fun!

"I make a game out of frugal supermarket shopping. I set a spending limit, say $100. I try to find the best deals on everything on my list to get as close as possible to my goal. Usually I get pretty close."

And finally . . .

"Stick to the list. Stick to the list. Stick to the list."

The Frugal Woman Knows...

BULK SHOPPING BASICS

Many Frugal Women have found joining a warehouse price club saves them money over the long term. But such places are not for the unwary. Here Frugal Women share their tips for avoiding spending in bulk when buying in bulk. Their top tip: When heading to a discount warehouse, make zipper-top resealable plastic bags the first item on your list, so that you can divvy up all your *other* bulk-size buys into manageable portions and store or freeze what you won't immediately use.

Break up the bulk.

"Don't buy large sizes of things you don't eat often or that might spoil before you can use it up. For example, I buy the large can of catsup, divide it up into canning jars, and keep it in the freezer or the fridge. It's a good deal for us because our family uses a lot of catsup, but you will have to decide what's right for your family. When we buy meat, we divide it up into meal-size portions and store them in the freezer. We buy meat only once every four to six weeks."

Check the unit prices.

"Warning: Sometimes bulk-size items may seem like bargains but they really aren't. To be sure you're getting the best deal you should compare unit prices. For example, my market sells a 96-ounce size bottle of orange juice, in addition to the normal 64-ounce size. You'd think the larger size would be the bargain, right? I realized that the larger one was twice the price, but only one and a half times the volume—not a bargain at all."

Buy it because you need it, not because it's cheap.

"Before going nuts, ask yourself a few things: Is this something I would buy and use anyway? Is the price low enough to make a difference? Do I have a place to store this? Will this go bad before I can use it up?"

Team up for savings.

"If you live alone or have a small family, team up with friends and buy in bulk. You all save money and nothing gets wasted."

TAME YOUR GROCERY BILLS WITH A GROCERY EXILE

Impulse buying doesn't just happen at the mall—it hits everywhere, even (or especially) at the grocery store. Give in enough times, and you'll have sky-high bills and a pantry full of "well, I'll use it some-day" food. Tame your bills and pare down your pantry stocks to the items you really need with a gro-cery exile—an ingenious exercise in self-discipline and creativity developed by some of the Frugal Women on iVillage. One exile participant explains:

The basic idea of a "grocery exile" is to use up some of the things that you already have on hand—items that might otherwise continue to languish in the back of the pantry while you replenish those often used items. There are a few ways to do it: Some people start by inventorying their supplies. Then they make up menus with what is available, and only go to the store to fill in with dairy and produce, for as long as it takes to get through all of the menus.

Others just pull out all of those "why did I buy that?" items and try to create recipes. Still others might swear off any nonperishable purchases except those that take advantage of a great sale on something they use regularly—it's up to you, whatever works best for you. That might be saving some money that otherwise would be spent on groceries and using it elsewhere. Or cleaning out some much needed room in your packed freezer or pantry. Or even seeing how creative you can be with what you've got.

The Frugal Woman Knows...

HOW TO BE A COUPON QUEEN

Snip, snip, snip. The Frugal Woman keeps her scissors close by when going through the Sunday paper. Here are some Frugal Women's best tips for using coupons to cut their grocery bills down to size.

Categorize those coupons.

"Organize your coupons by category so they are easy for you to find while at the store."

Don't get hung up on brands.

"I love coupons, but you can't let yourself remain loyal to any one brand. I don't have brand loyalty when it comes to health and beauty aids. Every week it's a different brand on sale."

Call for coupons.

"Call the 800 numbers for the companies that make all of the household products that you use: food, cleaning supplies, baby stuff, shampoos, and so on. You can find the numbers right on the packages. They are all quite happy to put you on mailing lists to receive coupons, recipe books, and more. You may be stuck on hold for a long time, but when you think of the money you can save it is well worth it."

Check out Websites.

"Try visiting manufacturer's Websites for your favorite products. Some will send you free coupons just for filling out a survey."

Double (and triple) your savings pleasure.

"If your supermarket offers double (or triple) coupon days, remember that they sell a lot more than just food. If you watch the sales carefully, you can take advantage of double coupon periods and stock up on necessities. I can often get items like toothpaste, deodorant, shampoo, trash bags, and sandwich bags for free—and they don't spoil so you don't have to worry about overbuying. I almost never buy store brands anymore, and it's not uncommon for me to save more than 50 percent on my grocery store bill."

The Frugal Woman Knows . . .

IF SHE DOESN'T NEED THAT COUPON, SOMEONE ELSE DOES (AND VICE VERSA)

You're studying this week's coupon circular from your Sunday paper, and only a few products you regularly use are featured. Don't get discouraged—and don't toss those other coupons! Start a coupon exchange instead.

Organize a few like-minded friends (even if they live in other towns or states) and exchange the coupons you have and don't want for the ones they don't need. One way to keep this moving is to do it chain-letter style, as one iVillage Frugal Woman describes. She says, "Try starting a coupon train. When you clip your coupons from the newspapers, keep what you want and mail the rest to the next person on the list. When the next person gets that package of coupons, they take what they want and put in all their coupons that they don't want, and so on. The batch of coupons keeps going down the list of addresses with some being pulled out, and more added at each stop. Don't forget to pull out the expired ones.

Coupon trains are great if you don't work at an office, or don't have any neighbors interested in trading."

Other ways to hunt down the discounts you most want, if you're willing to send off some that you don't: Check out online coupon swap groups, like the one found at iVillage's ParentsPlace at http://messageboards.ivillage.com/iv-ppcoupon.

WHERE THE COUPONS ARE

These days, you don't have to wait for the Sunday circular to get your weekly coupons. A simple search on Google.com for "coupons" will immediately give you about 100 links to sites offering national and local discounts. These are some of the most well-known and interesting out there.

Smartsource.com

Offers grocery-store coupons for national brands. Registration is free; you print the coupons from your computer. Plus when you register, you can opt to get weekly updates on savings sent to your email box.

Coolsavings.com

Offers savings on everything from grocery items to auto loans. Free registration lets you print coupons from your computer. Plus you'll get access to online-only discount offers, as well as the ability to browse weekly circulars from multiple big-name chains.

Valpak.com

From the same company that sends out local coupons by mail; simply enter your ZIP code to find online discount offers from local services and establishments.

Stonybrookfarms.com

This producer of natural and organic dairy products offers electronic coupons from 50 other natural and organic manufacturers, including Earth's Best Baby Foods, Annie's Naturals, and more.

RICH LIFE REWARDS:
A FRUGAL WOMAN'S TALE

Perhaps the greatest gift that I have given my children is the understanding that although money can provide happiness, laughter, and wonderful shopping experiences, the shortage or lack of money, by no means, eliminates these from our lives.

Some people may laugh at our weekly "garage sale-ing" in the summer, but this has become a very fond memory for my oldest daughter. We would get up very early, just the two of us, and sneak away for our shopping excursion. The find was not nearly as much fun as the hunt, but the conversations were even more rewarding. Just my daughter and me, $5 in my purse, and four hours of wonderful conversations and laughter.

Anyhow, sometimes I feel having less money can be so much more rewarding than too much money. And yes, my daughters have on occasion asked if we were poor. My answer has always been the same: "No, dear, we are not poor at all. Only broke." And they, bless their souls, know the difference.

—Monique Roffey, Winchester, Ontario, Canada

CHAPTER 3

◆

THE FRUGAL WOMAN Cooks

*A*t first, being frugal was a necessity, due to the fact that I lost my job. Soon, however, frugality became a way of life. I was excited to see that I could feed a family of five for only $40 a week without sacrificing the meals we loved. I was actually excited about going grocery shopping again, if you can believe that! Now the whole family gets involved in our frugal lifestyle. Even our kids have learned *to comparison shop to make sure they're getting the best bargain for their money.*

—Keri Belzer, Independence, Missouri

———————— ✦ ————————

HAVING TAKEN THE FRUGAL SHOPPING LESSONS OF Chapter 2 to heart, you may now be looking forward to your grocery shopping as a challenge rather than a chore. The next step on your path to enjoying the frugal life is conquering your kitchen. The number one rule: "Plan your meals based on what is on sale or inexpensive." You may have noticed that fruit and vegetables are cheaper when in season, for example. If you think you've read something along those lines in interviews with restaurant chefs, you're right. Shopping in season is just one of the principles the frugal home cook shares with gourmet chefs. Frugal cooking is not so much about living on packaged mac-and-cheese or Ramen Noodles, but about making the most of what's on hand and letting nothing go to waste.

The Frugal Woman Knows . . .

TO COOK LIKE HER GRANDMOTHER DID

Frugal Women have discovered that taking an "old-fashioned" approach to life in the kitchen helps make a little go a long way. From cutting down on prepackaged foodstuffs to stretching ingredients, following the cooking principles our foremothers used helps cut costs at the grocery store.

Make it yourself.

"Soup stock is easily made by boiling a chicken or turkey carcass (leftover, perhaps, from a weekend dinner) together with some vegetables. Even more frugal: Don't buy beautiful fresh vegetables for your stock; use the limp carrots and flaccid celery languishing in the back of your vegetable bin—you're just going to toss them after cooking. Gourmets everywhere will tell you to hang on to your vegetable peelings and trimmings as well (store in a zipper-top bag in the freezer), and use those as the base for soups."

———— ✦ ————

"Make cakes and brownies from scratch, instead of buying boxed mixes."

———— ✦ ————

"If you drink tea, hot cocoa, and so on, at work, instead of paying for hot drinks at the cafeteria or coffee shop, brew your own at your desk."

———— ✦ ————

"Try your hand at homemade bread. Bread machines are pretty inexpensive these days, and (barely) used ones can be had for cheap at garage sales or resale shops. Make in batches and freeze."

———— ✦ ————

"Instead of a pricey powdered mix, make your own iced tea. It costs about a penny a glass, and takes almost no effort: Fill a gallon container with water, add six to eight tea bags, and let steep in a sunny window or outside for several hours."

———— ✦ ————

"Make your own lemonade: To make lemonade syrup base, dissolve 1½ cups sugar in a half cup boiling water. Add the grated zest of one lemon and 1½ cups fresh lemon juice. Refrigerate in a covered container; stir one tablespoon per eight ounces of cold water for a refreshing glass of lemonade."

Eat healthfully to save money.

"Drink water. It costs less than soda, coffee, tea, and other drinks, and it is good for you! I bought one 1.5-liter bottle of water, drank it, washed out the bottle, and then refilled it with water (filtered in my Brita pitcher)."

———— ✦ ————

"Stop eating junk food (or at least cut back). It is more filling and less expensive to eat apples instead of potato chips, or carrot sticks instead of corn chips. It's healthier too."

Cook in bulk and freeze in portions.

"I do 'bulk freezer cooking.' Every two weeks or so, I scan the ads, see what's on sale, make lots of meals with those foods, and freeze them. Even if things get tough and I can't afford groceries, I always have plenty of meals in the freezer."

———— ✦ ————

"If you have freezer space, make your own spaghetti and pizza sauce, and cook beans from scratch. (Dry beans cost less than a dollar a pound, so cooking your own rather than buying canned makes sense.) Then freeze everything in meal-size portions."

Let nothing go to waste.

"If your recipe calls for one cup of diced onion, for instance, but your onion yields more than that cup, put the extra bits in a plastic yogurt container and freeze for later use."

MEAT DOES NOT MAKE THE MEAL

One way many Frugal Women cut down on food bills is to cut down on the amount of meat their families eat. As one says, "I try to think of meat as a condiment rather than the 'main event' of the meal." But you may have family members who balk at the idea of going vegetarian—even one night a week. Here are some ideas from Frugal Women for cutting back on meat without cutting it out altogether.

Set serving sizes.

Cut meat into individual serving size portions and freeze in individual bags (nutritionists will tell you that four ounces of raw meat or poultry—about the size of a deck of playing cards—constitutes a serving size). Thaw and cook only one serving for each person, so no one will be tempted by seconds. Serve more side dishes to round out your dinner. For instance, a pork chop resting on a large bed of sautéed cabbage and noodles and surrounded by colorful green beans and carrots looks like a gigantic portion of food.

Increase your veggies.

Reduce the amount of meat or poultry in your favorite casseroles and stews by half, and double up on the vegetables. You might try reducing the amount of beef in your chili, for instance, and add more beans and tomatoes.

Focus on taste.

Focus on making the food delicious, and no one will notice it has less meat—or even none at all. For example, a rich, well-seasoned lasagna made without meat, served with a big salad and crusty bread, is as likely to get rave reviews as its beef-packed cousin.

The Frugal Woman Knows...

"Spur of the Moment" Cooking
Wastes Time and Money

Even—or especially—if you are not a fan of cooking, taking an organized approach to meal planning can make dinner simpler, easier, and cheaper. Here is the story of one newly organized Frugal Woman.

It took me a few months to actually start planning our meals—and it really is the best thing that I could have done. We easily save 30 percent on grocery bills, and over the last two months we've ordered in or gone out for dinner only twice—and both were planned. In all honesty, I don't like cooking or looking at cookbooks, and have never paid much attention to the recipe section of magazines. However, I do like to save time, energy, and money.

Before I began meal planning, the phone calls would start after lunch: "What do you want for dinner?" "I don't know—what do *you* want?" "When do you get off—can *you* stop at the store and just grab something?" "No, I'm too tired; why don't you just order something in?" and so on. All very energy draining. Not having to think about it and having all the ingredients on hand makes me "feel like" eating whatever is on the menu for that night. Now my husband actually helps out with the meal planning!

Here's my method for creating a meal-planning system that even the kitchen-phobic can embrace.

1. My first step was to take a calendar and just write down what we had eaten over a four-week period. I found that most of our meals were the same thing or similar.

2. I then made a list of all the things that I can make that we enjoy to eat. (Trust me—it was a short list.)

3. The next step was to plan a menu for one week. That took forever—but I begrudgingly did it.

4. I then made a grocery list based on the menu. After one week of having meals and only going to the grocery store once, I was hooked.

5. I keep my calendars with our meals written on them for future reference (and to avoid having chili six times in one month).

6. I have "backup meals"—such as omelets or pasta with sauce—for days when we both end up working late.

The Frugal Woman Knows . . .
STOCKING UP CAN MEAN SAVINGS

Having an actual pantry—one big enough to accommodate multiple packages of basic supplies—will save you time and money. As one Frugal Woman advises, "Look for bargains on nonperishable items that you can stock up on. A well-stocked pantry can save you money because you won't have to run to the store at the last minute and risk paying higher prices."

Don't have a pantry? Set up shelves in a cool, dry area of your basement or kitchen, and begin stocking up whenever you find items on sale or when you visit a warehouse club.

Here are sample items to stock up on.

Dry Goods
Flour (all-purpose, cake, bread)
Cornmeal

Sugar (white, brown, confectioners')
Powdered milk
Baking powder
Baking soda
Oatmeal
Grits
Cereal
Raisins
Dried beans (at least three types)
Rice
Lentils
Pasta (spaghetti, macaroni, and at least two other types)
Spices
Dried herbs
Salt and pepper

Canned and Jarred Goods

Tuna
Corned beef
Applesauce
Peanut butter
Jelly or jam
Pancake syrup
Honey
Molasses
Corn syrup
Vegetable shortening
Olive oil
Vegetable oil
Vinegar (white, cider, wine)

Soy sauce

Worcestershire sauce

Vanilla extract

Canned tomatoes (puree and whole)

Tomato sauce

Tomato paste

Chicken broth

For a Rich Life...

START A KITCHEN GARDEN

One of the best ways to save on food bills and still have gourmet-quality produce is to grow your own (of course, you have to steel yourself against the urge to buy every garden gadget available). One Frugal Woman tells of her garden:

We raise tomatoes, green beans, squash, cucumbers, onions, peppers, and potatoes. We usually raise enough potatoes to last us all winter! We eat about 10 pounds a week, so that is a huge savings for us. During the summer we always have fresh veggies and I can the extra to eat all winter. If you don't know how to can, you can always freeze them.

I even have two peach trees and a grapevine that I use to make jelly for the kids. I love having the fresh stuff right out in the yard all summer, and being able to preserve it over the winter too. Even if you don't have room for a garden, you can probably get started with a container garden on your porch or patio.

Take it slowly at first. See what grows well in your area. Then you can expand the next year. Plant only things that you know your family will eat. Remember that you can do many things with the produce you grow, besides eating it fresh. If you grow cucumbers, for instance, you can make pickles. If you grow tomatoes, you can make salsa and spaghetti sauce. And so on.

FRUGAL WOMAN, FRUGAL WOMAN, HOW DOES YOUR GARDEN GROW? ORGANICALLY, OF COURSE.

Organic gardening—growing plants without chemical pesticides, herbicides, or fertilizers—saves money, protects the earth, and makes the produce you grow safer for your family. Who can argue with that?

As one Frugal Woman explains, "We kill weeds by just pulling them up. We use compost to enrich the soil. We pick off insects or use soapy water to kill them." Here are some other Frugal Women's tips on having a *green* green thumb.

Recycle, recycle, recycle.

"I layer black-and-white newsprint with my compost and other organic material, saving money while enriching my soil. I use plastic soda bottles as mini-greenhouses (cut the bottles in half and place them over seedlings) and as part of a watering system in my garden and for my houseplants."

Create a compost pile.

"Variety is the key to composting. Use lawn clippings, brown stuff like leaves and twigs, old mulch, shredded paper, or wood chips. Use food scraps like coffee grounds, greens, old yuck from the bottom of the produce drawer, and banana peels,. Put in a scoop of good fertile dirt once in a while, so the microscopic critters can go to work in your compost. Rabbit, horse, and other herbivore manure is great if you can find it, but avoid dog or cat droppings."

Save on water bills with a rain barrel.

"If you're starting a garden, buy a garbage can and turn it into a rain barrel. Use that water to water your garden. I even catch the condensation from my air conditioner in the summer in a bucket to reuse. There is an outside water ban in our region, so it really helps. And it saves us money on our water bills." *[Editor's note: If you are considering your own water barrel for garden use, look into Mosquito Control Rings, available at many natural gardening supply stores, to prevent mosquitoes from breeding in the water.]*

The Frugal Woman Knows...

TO BUY PRODUCE IN SEASON

These days it seems like you can get any fruit or vegetable any time of year. How can the supermarket sell summer squashes in the dead of winter? Because of improved shipping methods, a lot of produce comes from halfway around the world (literally). For example, when it's winter in North America, it's summer in South America. But just because it's possible to get asparagus and strawberries all year round, that doesn't mean it's a frugal idea—buying produce "out of season" is typically more expensive—and fruits and vegetables are usually tastier when purchased closer to their natural season in your area. The solution: Stock up on your favorite fruits and vegetables and preserve them through freezing or drying. (Gardeners facing bumper crops will also find these ideas useful.) Here are some Frugal Women's ideas for making one season's bounty last all year long.

Broccoli and Cauliflower

"Before you begin, have a large colander and a large bowl of ice water ready. Also, have zipper-top plastic bags or sealable freezer containers at hand. Bring a large pot of water to a rolling boil—you want the broccoli and cauliflower to float freely, so use plenty of water. Cut the vegetables into similar-size pieces. For broccoli, you want to split the really large stems because the 'flower' part cooks so fast. Once the water is boiling, add about a tablespoon of salt per gallon, then drop in the broccoli or cauliflower. For the broccoli I usually boil for three minutes, no more. For cauliflower, five or six minutes. Lift the vegetables out or pour through a colander, then put the colander into the ice water and swish around to quickly cool the vegetables and stop the cooking. Lift the colander from the ice water and allow to drain well. Portion into bags or containers and seal well. If using plastic bags, you can use a straw to suck out the excess air. The less air in the container the better the product will be when it is used. Pop those bags into the freezer, ready for you to fix later. To cook the frozen vegetables, bring a one- or two-quart pot of water to a boil. Drop the frozen vegetables in and cook quickly. I also cook them in the microwave with just a few spoonfuls of water with good results."

Garlic

"Garlic can be preserved for a long time in the freezer. Just separate the cloves, without peeling, and place in a freezer container."

Fresh Herbs

"There are several ways to dry fresh herbs. They can be picked on long stems, tied loosely, and hung upside down until they are dry. If you gently strip off the fresh leaves and spread them on paper towels they will dry nicely too, but both these methods take up space and also take a long time. The other disadvantage to slow drying is they may get dusty. To dry them in the oven, wash and air-dry the herbs, strip off the leaves, and spread in a single layer on baking sheets. Put in a warm oven overnight and most will be dry enough to package by morning."

———— ✦ ————

"You can also freeze your herbs. Chives, thyme, and parsley can be snipped or chopped, put in a plastic container, and frozen just like that. When you need some, just scrape them out with the tines of a fork. For basil, I usually whiz it in the blender with olive oil, and freeze it in an ice cube tray, because the leaves turn black when frozen and the oil keeps them nice and green. When the cubes are frozen I pop them out and put them in plastic freezer bags. The cubes can be thawed and made into pesto. I do this with marjoram and oregano too."

———— ✦ ————

"Here is a solution to the dust problem with air-drying herbs. I tie the fresh herbs into little bunches, poke a little hole in the bottom of a plastic baggie, and slip the stems through. Tie the bag where the stems are gathered and tied, and hang them upside down. The air can still get at them but the dust won't settle on the leaves."

———— ✦ ————

"You'll never need to throw away unused fresh parsley again—you can dehydrate it. Place the parsley in a single layer on a paper towel on a dinner plate and microwave it for several minutes, opening the door and turning the parsley over a couple of times until it seems dry to the touch. Let it sit on the counter until thoroughly cool, then crumble the dried leaves onto another plate. Throw away all the stem and stem pieces. Transfer the dried parsley into a container and store with your other spices in the cupboard. It stays bright green if you don't continue cooking it after it is dry."

Lemons

"Juice a bunch of lemons, strain out the seeds, and put the juice in ice cube trays. When frozen, pop out the cubes and store them in a zipper-top plastic bag. Thaw out a cube anytime a recipe calls for fresh lemon juice. This will of course work with any citrus juice."

———— ✦ ————

"Whole lemons should never be frozen. The juice sacs burst. When the fruit thaws, the pulp often will be dry and mushy. Instead, separately freeze the juice, grated zest, and reamed-out shells to use as containers."

———— ✦ ————

"To dry lemon zest, grate zest and spread in a single a layer on a baking sheet. Dry in a 200°F oven for one hour. Cool; store in covered container. Six tablespoons fresh grated zest, from about six lemons, will dry to three tablespoons zest. Use in potpourri or mix with coarsely ground black pepper for seasoning."

Onions

"Onions bought in bulk save a lot of money, as long as you use them up before they go bad. Here's a method for keeping them fresh longer. You take old panty hose (laundered), and drop an onion into one leg. Tie a knot above the onion and drop in another until you have a double string of them. Cut off the panty part and tie the whole thing. Then hang the hose on a hook in a cool dark place. When you need an onion, just cut off the lowest one below the knot, and the knot will hold the next one in place. My onions are still nice after a whole month. The nylons insure a flow of air around the onions, keeping them from getting moist and molding."

Peppers and Chiles

"Try roasting and freezing peppers and chiles. Roast them either on the grill or under the broiler until the skin turns blackened all over. Transfer to a brown paper bag and twist the top shut. Let sit until cool, then scrape off the blackened skin, take out the seeds and cut them up. You can store them in jars in the refrigerator, or freeze in small containers."

Potatoes

"You can freeze potatoes if they're at least partially cooked and not in too much liquid. Here's a recipe for freezing shredded potatoes. You can use these to make hash browns, potato pancakes (latkes), or anything that calls for chopped potato. Peel the potatoes and shred into a bowl of cold water (to prevent from turning brown—they turn really fast when you shred). Rinse and let soak in clean, salted water for a short while to break down the starchiness. Drain well and spread onto a cookie sheet or jelly roll pan and bake in a 325°F oven until just starting to look dry, about 30 minutes. You want to just partially cook them. Let cool and transfer to plastic containers or zipper-top plastic bags for freezer storage."

Tomatoes

"To freeze tomatoes, first drop them into boiling water for a minute to loosen the skins. Plunge into cold water, slip off the skins, then, working over a strainer, cut in half and squirt out the seeds into the strainer. Cut the tomatoes into pieces and pack in freezer containers. They are very fresh tasting when they thaw."

———— ✦ ————

"Sun-dried tomatoes are expensive to buy, but you can make your own when tomatoes are in season. You will need nice, firm, ripe tomatoes with no bruises. The best tomatoes for drying are Roma or Italian plum tomatoes, but you can use any kind. Wash the tomatoes and dry them. If using small plum tomatoes, just cut them in half lengthwise. For larger ones, cut thick lengthwise slices. Arrange on a cookie sheet and put them in a warm oven, no more than 200°F, or lower if possible. Leave them in the oven overnight and check in the morning. Turn and continue drying until they are leathery. Of course, if you have a food dehydrator the job is even simpler. They are best stored in an airtight container in the refrigerator."

Winter Squash

"This works well for pumpkin, acorn squash, or butternut squash. Wash them off, cut open, and scoop out the seeds. Cut into big chunks, place on a cookie sheet, and bake in a preheated 350°F oven until the flesh can be pierced easily with a fork. Remove from the oven and let cool thoroughly. Take a large spoon, remove the flesh, and discard the skin. You can now put the pumpkin or squash in zipper-top freezer bags. Remove as much air as you can, close, and flatten the bags down somewhat so they store easily stacked in the freezer. This will keep fine for a year but is best used within nine months. It's ready to thaw anytime and use in pies, cookies, muffins, soups, or a hot side dish. Use butternut or acorn squash in pies, muffins, and quick breads in place of pumpkin. People won't know the difference if you don't tell them."

The Frugal Woman Knows...

TO STRETCH FOODS' FRESHNESS
THROUGH PROPER STORAGE

It's great to stock up on foods at the warehouse club or when the supermarket runs a special, but if they're perishable, you may find yourself tossing more than you use. No Frugal Woman likes to see food go to waste, so the ability to extend the life of perishable items is a skill worth acquiring.

Ground Beef

"Sometimes you buy a bulk-size package of ground beef, and once it's frozen, you realize you can't use it all at once. It does help if you can divide it up into portions, wrap and label before freezing, but we don't always have time, do we? Here's my solution: You can refreeze the beef as long as you cook it first, and then package it into meal-size portions. Cooking it well will kill any bacteria that may have developed as it thawed. The danger comes when you thaw food, because a few bacteria are always waiting to develop as the food warms up. Then if you refreeze it without cooking it first, the next time you thaw it, those bacteria will be ready and waiting to multiply."

Milk

"When you have milk that is nearing the expiration date, pour the milk into an ice cube tray and freeze it. When the milk cubes are frozen, you can place them in a zipper-top plastic bag and keep them in the sealed bag in the freezer. Then, when you have tea or coffee, pull out a milk cube. It will help cool the coffee down too. These cubes are also good for cooling down hot cream soups."

Cheese

"When I buy a big piece of semi-soft cheese (cheddar, Jack, mozzarella), I cut it into portions that will be used up quickly. I wrap each portion tightly in plastic wrap then tightly in aluminum foil. I put my wrapped pieces in a labeled zipper-top plastic bag and put it in the freezer. I find that the double wrapping eliminates air and prevents freezer burn. The pieces thaw quickly and can even be grated while frozen."

———— ✦ ————

"For sliced cheese in the original vacuum package, you can keep the unopened package in the freezer for a few months. However, if the cheese is not separated by paper or plastic between the slices, then the slices stick together when they thaw."

Oils

"Olive oil, walnut oil, and other oils have a tendency to go rancid fairly quickly if left in a warm place or in sunlight. Buy some decorative bottles with corks and opaque bottles (ceramic is good). Transfer your oils from their glass or clear plastic containers into the new bottles, and label the bottles with a permanent marker."

Applesauce

"Have you ever had a jar of applesauce in the fridge that was moldy on top? Just store applesauce upside down and it will last four times as long. Don't ask me how, but it does."

For a Rich Life . . .

TURN LEFTOVERS INTO COMFORT FOOD FEASTS

Half a roasted chicken. A few slices of baked ham. So good the first time around, but what are you going to do with them now? Using up leftovers doesn't just mean reheating Tuesday night's dinner on Thursday. In fact, dozens of our favorite comfort foods—from split pea soup to chicken pot pie—have their origin in "leftovers." Here are some Frugal Women's favorite ways to make the "second time around" as good as the first.

Rump Roast

"Slice rump roast before freezing in portion sizes. I like to make roast beef hash—just finely dice cooked potatoes, onion, and meat; form the mixture into patties; and fry until very crisp on the outside."

"Use leftover roast beef for sandwiches, beef stroganoff, or beef stew. Whatever you do, slice it first. Consider dividing up your roast into a couple of containers so that when the urge strikes, you only have to defrost one container. One more idea—sliced beef and gravy on bread, open faced, with mashed potatoes."

———— ✦ ————

"Take the leftover roast and place it in a slow cooker. Add the contents of a bottle of your favorite barbecue sauce. Add a teaspoon each of garlic powder, onion powder, and salt. Set the slow cooker on low or high, depending on how long you need to cook it."

Meatloaf

"Meatloaf sandwiches: Take a thin slice of meatloaf, put it on some good bread, and add the condiments of your choice (pickles, onion, lettuce, tomato)."

———— ✦ ————

"Meatloaf Parmesan: Slice what's left of the meatloaf and layer it in a baking pan along with tomato sauce. Top with mozzarella cheese and bake until heated through and the cheese is bubbly."

Steak

"Have leftover steak cold, sliced thin, tossed in a salad or in sandwiches. Or cut it in pieces and make a one-dish rice casserole. Sauté some onions, toss in the meat and canned tomatoes, then mix it with cooked rice and top with shredded cheese and bake it. Or how about fajitas? Slice thin while still cold, toss in a skillet with sliced onion and pepper, and serve wrapped in flour tortillas with salsa."

Ham

"To freeze, cut the ham off the bone, remove the rind, and break up into manageable portions. Place in zipper-top freezer bags and freeze. To use the leftovers, add some to boxed macaroni and cheese with a handful of frozen peas. Or add some to packaged Ramen Noodle soup with a couple of handfuls of frozen mixed vegetables. You can add it to potato salad, macaroni salad, or pasta salad. Add it to scrambled eggs, with or without cheese. Ham is great in split pea soup, which is incredibly easy and economical to make from scratch. Ham is great in just about any bean dish. It is also a great topper for twice-baked potatoes, along with cheese, broccoli, and whatever else you would want to add. Just about any soup you can think of will taste great with ham in it."

——— ✦ ———

"If your ham has a bone, don't forget to save it for soup. You can use it for split pea, lentil, bean, or potato soup, starting with ham stock. To make ham stock, put the ham bone in a soup pot with a carrot, an onion, and a stalk of celery, all cut in pieces, and a bay leaf. Add water to cover by about two inches and bring to a boil. Reduce the heat to a slow simmer, cover, and simmer for at least two hours. Remove the bone, reserving any bits of meat, strain out the vegetables, skim the fat, and you've got the base for delicious soup."

——— ✦ ———

"Potato and ham casserole: Boil two cups diced potatoes until tender. Layer in a casserole dish with one cup diced ham on top. Melt a quarter cup of margarine in a saucepan; add three tablespoons of flour, stir, then add one and a half cups of milk. Stir to thicken, add a little salt and pepper, and pour over the ham and potatoes. Top with a quarter cup of bread crumbs and a half cup of grated cheddar cheese. Bake in a preheated 350°F oven for about 20 minutes, or until browned."

Chicken and Turkey

"Inside-out chicken pot pie: This is a good, but cheap, recipe for leftover chicken. Use as much or as little chicken as you want. Simply take the meat off the bones and cut up into bite-size pieces. Add the chicken to a can of cream of chicken soup and combine with one 16-ounce package of frozen vegetables. Transfer to a pot and simmer until the vegetables are tender. Make biscuits to serve on the side."

———— ♦ ————

"Turkey hash: In a large bowl, combine equal amounts of finely diced turkey and finely diced cooked potatoes (or use frozen hash browns). Add minced onion, finely diced green or red bell pepper, and salt and pepper to taste. Mix everything together well. In a large, heavy skillet, heat a tablespoon or two of vegetable oil until sizzling. Turn the turkey mixture into the hot skillet. Press down with the back of a spatula and brown over medium-high heat. When the bottom is browned, turn the other side to brown by turning in sections or by flipping out onto a plate and sliding back into the pan. The hash can also be formed into patties and fried for individual servings."

———— ♦ ————

"My family's favorite is barbecued turkey sandwiches. Just throw some shredded turkey in a pot with your favorite barbecue sauce and simmer. Also keep in mind that you can freeze your shredded leftover turkey and thaw it out in a couple of weeks for another meal."

Noodles and Pasta

"Combine leftover noodles or pasta with cottage cheese, eggs beaten with milk, apricot preserves, and raisins; pour into a greased baking dish; and bake at 350°F until set. The amounts are not really crucial—just make sure the noodles are well coated with the egg custard. It's delicious for dessert, breakfast, or for a side dish."

Bread

"Homemade bread crumbs: Let your leftover bread sit out a little while to dry and then run it through the food processor. You could also use a blender. Put the crumbs in a zipper-top plastic bag and keep them in the freezer. (I also put old bread in the freezer to make up the crumbs—when I have a lot, out comes the food processor.)"

———— ✦ ————

"Here's another option for homemade bread crumbs. To dry out the bread, put it in the toaster (or on a cookie sheet in the oven if you have a lot) and take it out when it's dry but not yet toasted."

———— ✦ ————

"Remember to use your leftover hot dog and hamburger buns for homemade bread crumbs too."

Halloween Candy

"This is a great way to use up all the candy your kids have brought home, and an easy bake-sale treat: Take the chocolate and peanut butter candy (such as Reese's peanut butter cups), plain chocolate (such as Hershey's Kisses or plain bars), and crispy rice bars (such as Nestlé Crunch), unwrap them, and put them in a heavy saucepan with a little oil over low heat. Add some crunchy peanut butter and some chocolate chips, and melt all of it until smooth. Next, add a few cups of crisped rice cereal, and stir until everything is evenly coated. Drop rounded tablespoons of the mixture onto a metal cookie sheet, and transfer to the freezer for a few minutes to help them set. Serve at room temperature."

———— ✦ ————

"Put leftover Halloween candy in small baggies for trips to the movies. Each family member gets one bag, so you control the portion size of the sweets. This also saves you a trip to the overpriced concession stand."

———— ✦ ————

"For a creative topping for ice cream sundaes, chop up assorted leftover Halloween chocolates."

No Matter What You've Got: Frugal Fried Rice

This is an "add what's in your fridge" recipe. It's good in its most basic form and even better with additions. In a large skillet or wok over medium heat, add one tablespoon oil, four cups cooked rice, one chopped onion, two stalks celery (chopped), and one teaspoon chopped garlic. Cook, stirring, over medium heat for a minute or two. Add two tablespoons soy sauce and four beaten eggs, and stir-fry until eggs are scrambled. Serve hot with additional soy sauce. You can add any of the following leftovers: shrimp, tuna, chicken, salmon, turkey, plus chopped vegetables such as mushrooms, peas, green beans, and zucchini.

RICH LIFE REWARDS:
A FRUGAL WOMAN'S TALE

When I was growing up, my family didn't have a lot of money to spare on eating out or buying many new things. My mom didn't work until my brother was in kindergarten. I remember her buying food in bulk and freezing it in smaller portions, making meals to be frozen for times when my dad was out of town on business, so she would have fast healthy meals ready to go for the three small children she was raising.

We also always had a garden and many of our fruits and vegetables came from there. She would carefully blanch and freeze the vegetables and can the fruits so that we would have healthy inexpensive meals in the wintertime and ready-to-go veggies to go with her previously prepared meals. I remember it being a ritualistic process at the waning of every summer where we would all go out to the garden and harvest the green beans, peas, tomatoes, zucchini, corn, cabbages, and other vegetables that she experimented with. We would then help her to blanch and put them into freezer bags and carry them to the deep freeze in the basement.

Now, as an adult, I look back at this and I see that it was much more than saving money. It was spending time together as a family, laboring together as a family, and saving money and (later) time as a family. Frugality means many things to many people. To me, frugality is a home-cooked meal, laundry dried in the sun, and a family that turns off the TV and sits down to dinner together to share stories of the day. It is a sacrifice for the betterment of the family. Frugal is the feel of home and the experience of family.

—Taycia Yockim, Thornton, Colorado

CHAPTER 4

◆

THE FRUGAL WOMAN
Organizes, Cleans, and Saves Energy

*B*eing frugal and being organized go hand in hand. Being organized saves so much money and time—and time, well, we could all be a little more frugal with our time. So now I am totally organized and have more free time to spend with my family and myself. By being frugal, there is no worry about debt collectors or feeling small and dirty

*because you can't pay a bill. If you don't owe anyone any-
more, or you stay caught up and don't go into any more
debt, it is such a feeling of freedom—what MasterCard
would call "priceless!" It is a whole new way of life that
would make our country even better, if we all caught on to
this concept: being organized and utilizing what we have,
not what we think we need or want, frees us up to be able
to get what we need.*

—Nancy Hutchins, Herrin, Illinois

THE FRUGAL WOMAN'S HOME IS, FOR THE MOST PART,
a simpler home. She doesn't need the newest this or trendiest that, when her current one works just as well. But that doesn't mean she lives a purely spartan existence. In fact, the Frugal Woman's home is one of the places her economy-minded
creativity truly shines through. Combine household organization with frugality,
and you might rediscover a closet (or even a room!) you'd given up for lost.
Through frugal measures, you can cut your spending on pricey household cleaners and still have a sparkling clean house (plus do some good for the earth in the
bargain). And cutting your energy bills—well, who wouldn't want to write a
smaller check to the power company each month?

Organizing Your Home

The Frugal Woman Knows...

Organization Is the Answer— to Everything

No two principles are as closely intertwined as frugality and organization. Simply put, it's just plain impossible to live frugally over the long term without getting organized. And conversely, getting organized is what helps many women take their first step toward frugality—once they get everything they don't need out of their life, they wonder why they let in all that junk in the first place. And that helps cut down on the urge to impulse buy!

Organization, as we've seen in previous chapters, applies to everything from how you handle your money to how you approach shopping. In this section, we'll deal specifically with home organization and how it can help you pare your life (and stuff) down to the most important parts.

The Frugal Woman Knows...

TO BE FRUGAL WITH THE SPACE SHE'S GOT

As overwhelmed with "stuff" as many of us are, it's perennially tempting to believe that just one more closet or room would be the answer to our space conundrums. But Frugal Women know they (usually) don't need an extra room in their homes; they just need to clear out the ones they've got. As one Frugal Woman said when contemplating the contents of her kitchen hutch, "There is a lot of stuff in there I never use. What a waste of good space this has been—I've been thinking how to reclaim that space and make it functional!"

Wasted space is, in fact, wasted money—just think of the value of the square feet (or even inches) clutter is taking up in your home. A round of de-cluttering may also change your feelings about what you really need in life. As another Frugal Woman exclaimed after embracing a more organized life, "I'm tired of junk. I used to think that we needed a lot of 'things,' but that just isn't true. My motto is, 'If you haven't used it in a year, you probably never will. So get rid of it!'"

Organizing a whole house—or even a whole room—can be a daunting task. And it's not necessary to take it on in one day, one week, or even one month. Frugal Women—as conscious of the value of their time as of their money—recommend following these three principles as you move through clearing out your drawers, cabinets, and progressively, your home as a whole.

Find focus spots.

"I took a good look at my life, my expectations, and my dreams—such as they are—and realized that I really and truly hate my computer area. It's a mess all the time and therefore makes the whole room look a mess. So that became one of my focus spots for the year. I then realized when I was trying to fix supper one night, that my counters did not allow me to do any work. That then became focus spot number two. Then I opened the refrigerator and stuff fell out. That became the third spot to focus on. Then I can move on to other areas."

Attack clutter in an organized way.

"The trick is to have boxes or bags ready for the stuff so you won't just be creating piles that don't make any sense. I put out a throw-away bag, a give-to-younger-cousins bag, and a give-to-thrift-shop bag. And of course there is a keep bag. As I go through stuff, I try not to think about any one item too long. I just pick it up and toss it in the appropriate bag. I try to be ruthless."

Don't bring clutter back in.

"When I do go shopping, I ask myself, 'Where would I put it?' Ninety-nine percent of the time, I put the item back down."

For a Rich Life . . .

APPRECIATE THE PEACE THAT
COMES WITH PARING DOWN

The simple life has its own rewards, as many a Frugal Woman can attest. Not least on the list of benefits is less stress—freeing oneself from the burden of extra stuff that clutters the mind, soul, and home. And as you progress down the path to simplicity, you'll likely discover that there are others walking the same route. One Frugal Woman points out, "The biggest change in the way I do things is that

I am conscious of what I am doing or not doing. I'm able to appreciate what I've done and what accomplishments I've made. It's changing my way of thinking about a lot of things. That said, I think it's very important to be able to appreciate even the smallest accomplishment in this journey. Each one is important and builds on the last. When you stop and look with pride at what you've done, and remember what it used to be, you are not being self-centered or vain. You are rejoicing in an accomplishment that goes beyond the actual cleaning, organizing, and reclaiming of space. It becomes spiritual. Your environment becomes part of you, and you a part of it. It is no longer just a house or an apartment. It becomes a home. Your self-esteem and confidence increase. Getting organized is about much more than just getting our 'stuff' organized. We are getting our mind, body, and soul organized as well. I can't live in regret for the years I've lost to clutter and disorganization. But I can begin to improve myself and my environment for today and tomorrow. Each day *can* be better than the last."

Another found that meeting with a group helps keep her life simple. She explains, "After years of reading about 'voluntary simplicity' and frugality, I found that many people were organizing groups of like-minded people to study ideas for minimizing their expenditures and maximizing their lives. Six months ago, I started a group with two other women. We meet twice a month at my house to discuss ways to save money and live more ecologically. The group has been steadily growing in size, and so has our commitment to enjoy life with less material baggage. It's easier to be frugal when you know you're not alone. Why not try to start a group in your neighborhood?"

CLEANING

The Frugal Woman Knows...

IT SHOULDN'T COST AS MUCH TO CLEAN HER HOME AS IT DID TO BUY IT

For as long as there have been women—Frugal or not—there have been cleaning products. Yes, even before the supermarket carried 17 different cleaners for your windows alone. Going back to the days when a few simple supplies sufficed, Frugal Women have been coming up with their own cleaners that really work. As one Frugal Woman comments, "Household cleaners are big business. Every week we spend millions on cleaners that are specialized or do-it-all. Look under your cabinet (or wherever you keep them) and count how many cleaners you have. Five, ten, more? Now look at why you bought them. Does one have the disinfecting power of bleach? Why not just use bleach? How about the one with the power of baking soda? Use plain soda! I'm sure you see where I'm going with this."

Yes, we do. Here's how to make some basic household cleansers that real Frugal Women swear by.

All-Purpose Quick Shiner

This shiner is mild and safe to use for all surfaces.

1¼ cups white vinegar
1¼ cups water

Pour the vinegar and water into a clean 22-ounce spray bottle. Shake gently to combine. To use, spray on and wipe off.

All-Purpose Cleaner

2 cups rubbing alcohol (70 percent isopropyl)
1 tablespoon mild dishwashing liquid (for handwashing dishes, not dishwasher detergent)
1 tablespoon ammonia
2 quarts water

In a large bowl or clean bucket, stir all ingredients together. Fill a clean spray bottle (not a recycled one) with the cleaner and store the rest tightly sealed in a large bottle. Use with a cloth or sponge to clean bathroom fixtures, kitchen fixtures, appliances, chrome, plastic countertops, and painted surfaces. Rinse with a clean cloth or sponge after cleaning.

Window and Glass Cleaner 1

¼ cup white vinegar
1 quart water

Pour the vinegar and water into a clean spray bottle. Shake gently to combine. Spray directly on windows and wipe clean.

Window and Glass Cleaner 2

"I've used just about every glass cleaner on the market and this is the only mix that really cleans streak-free and is inexpensive. I keep a sprayer bottle full, ready for glass spot-cleaning."

1 gallon water
1 cup ammonia
1 pint rubbing alcohol
2 tablespoons dish soap (Dawn brand is recommended)

Combine in a large, clean plastic container, and fill a spray bottle as needed.

Low-Sudsing Laundry Detergent

One 5.5-ounce bar of Fels Naptha Soap
1 box, plus 1 cup, Arm & Hammer Super Washing Soda
4 cups cold water
3 gallons hot tap water

In a large pot, grate the bar of Fels Naptha Soap. Add 4 cups of water, stir, and cook over low heat, stirring constantly, until all the grated soap is dissolved. Don't let it come to a boil.

Pour the mixture into a 5-gallon bucket and add 3 gallons of hot tap water. Stir until dissolved, then stir in 1 cup of washing soda (more if you have hard water). Mix well, then leave overnight to set up into a gel. Stir before using. Use ¾ cup (that's *two cents'* worth) for top-loading machines; use ⅛ cup for front-loading machines. Adjust as necessary for your particular needs. Larger machines and heavily soiled laundry will require more.

Automatic Dishwasher Detergent

"Most frugal experts, as well as 'green earth' experts, recommend using equal parts borax and baking soda in your dishwasher. If you have very hard water, use a little more soda as it's a water softener. For spotless rinses, try filling your rinse compartment with about one cup (don't overfill) of white vinegar (my favorite new cleaning fluid). If you feel you must use automatic dishwasher soap, buy the cheapest you can find and then add baking soda to it before washing."

Soft-Scrubbing Cleanser Alternative

"Those 'soft' cleansers are great because you can use them on all kinds of surfaces without worrying about scratching. However, the price isn't so great. Here is an idea for a substitute: Use lemon juice and baking soda to make a paste, and rub gently. Of course, you should test a patch first to make sure the surface won't be scratched, but generally it works for all bathroom surfaces. I also use this in my kitchen on and around the stove. The baking soda is just abrasive enough to scrub up yucky stuff, and the lemon bleaches porcelain back to white."

Drain Uncloggers

"If your kitchen drain is acting a little clogged, boil a quart of water with one cup of white vinegar added. Pour the boiling hot liquid down the drain and wait five minutes. If the clog was caused by grease, it should be cleared."

———— ✦ ————

"Pour bleach down a clogged drain and let it sit overnight. Run the hottest water down the drain and it should clear any clogs. I use the following method as a preventive measure for avoiding clogged drains: I pour bleach in every drain I have in the house once a month (about a cup or so). Don't run water down the drain for a couple of minutes. You will not have a clogging problem again. Remember to be cautious and safe around little hands and also protect yourself by wearing gloves and avoid splashing the bleach! I know it has high risks, but if you keep safety in mind, clogged drains will be a thing of the past."

White Vinegar to Whiten Clothes

"I use about half a cup of white vinegar per normal load of laundry. There's some vinegar smell during the wash cycle, but it fades in the dryer or on the line. Whites come out really white, and I find that my closets don't smell as musty. I also use it in a spray bottle as I would use a stain remover. Vinegar has lots of uses, and you can buy it by the gallon, for less than a dollar."

Meat Tenderizer to Remove Spit-Up Stains

"This is invaluable if you have a newborn in the family. The main cleaning ingredient I keep on hand in the laundry room is unflavored meat tenderizer. Mix it into a paste with water and rub it into any formula or milk stains, and the enzymes eat away the protein which causes the stain. It doesn't harm the fabric's colors. It's great for all those unpleasant stains from spitting up. Let it sit on the stain for about 10 minutes, and then launder as usual. My baby's bibs always looked new."

WD-40 for Oily Stains

"I keep a can of WD-40 in the laundry room. Sometimes you get those oily stains that have already been laundered and sit in from the dryer, so this really helps. Spray the oily stain with WD-40 and let it sit for 10 minutes (the oil reactivates the old oil). Then rub in some dish soap to help release the oil, and launder as usual. This will work very well if your husband does a lot of work in the garage."

Dryer Sheet Alternative

"Dryer sheets can get expensive over the years. Here's an alternative. Purchase a small bottle of generic liquid fabric softener. Put one cup of the softener in a container with one cup of water. Cut a four-by-six-inch sponge into four squares.

Soak the sponge in the mixture. When you do laundry, just throw an unsqueezed sponge into the dryer. My clothes smell better and there is less static than when I was using dryer sheets. When the clothes are dry, just toss the sponge back into the mixture. When the mixture runs out, just make more. The softener costs me $2.26. The bottle lasts me about a year."

Cornstarch as Spray Starch

"Add a tablespoon of cornstarch to a clean spray bottle and add water. Use it in place of spray starch the next time you iron. You'll save some money, and that's one less spray can in a landfill somewhere to clutter up this beautiful earth. It works so much better than spray starch too."

THE FRUGAL WOMAN'S CLEANING SUPPLIES

Stock up on the following ingredients to make the cleaners listed in this section.

Baking soda

White vinegar

Bleach

Ammonia

Isopropyl (rubbing) alcohol

Borax (available at most hardware stores)

Mild dishwashing liquid

The Frugal Woman Knows...

NATURAL CLEANERS WORK AS WELL

AS CHEMICAL ONES

There's no need to bring chemical-laden products into your home in order to get it sparkling clean. Natural—and cheap—cleansing compounds do the job just as well, and in a nontoxic manner. Here are 10 fresh solutions for getting your home clean, naturally.

1. "For disinfecting, mix half a cup of borax in one gallon of hot water. Use on counters, floors, cabinets, and tiles."

2. "Make your own furniture polish by adding half a cup of lemon juice to one cup of vegetable or olive oil."

3. "To beat mildew, use equal parts vinegar and salt. Or use strong thyme tea."

4. "Vinegar cleans everything. It is especially valuable against mold, like on the rim of the refrigerator and in the corners of the bathtub."

5. "Use borax to cut calcium on shower doors from hard water, and it's an excellent abrasive when mixed as a paste with either bleach or ammonia, or with just plain water."

6. "Spray the tub and shower daily with straight rubbing alcohol—this cuts way down on scrubbing."

7. "After a zillion professional steam cleanings, the guy 'came clean' and told me that the best stuff to use on your carpets is white vinegar. It acts like a cleaner and leaves no residue (like detergents) for future dirt to cling to. I have been

doing it ever since he told me. You can put the vinegar in the tank with your hot water, one or two cups per two gallons of water. The only drawback is the one or two hours of the house smelling like a salad, but it goes away. I especially like this because I have a nine-month-old, and who wants the chemicals on their carpet?"

8. "If you spill a liquid on your carpet like fruit punch or grape soda, while it's still wet, pour some salt on it. The salt soaks it right up. Let the salt do its job—leave it on the stain overnight. Then vacuum it up. Also, white wine neutralizes red wine, so pour some white wine on a red wine stain to get out the red, though it works best on just-spilled stains."

9. "If you are having trouble with ants in your house, find where they are coming in, rub your finger across the ant trail (they'll be discombobulated from losing the scent of the trail), and sprinkle instant grits in their path. They'll carry the grits back into the nest, the colony will eat it and then drink water, and the grits swell to kill them. Keep some sprinkled around the edges of your walls until you don't see ants anymore. Just make sure they are 'instant' and not 'fast cooking.' This method might take longer than hiring an exterminator, but it's much safer, and cheaper too. And it doesn't hurt the environment."

10. "To deal with moths, take some old panty hose with runs, and cut off the legs. Fill each leg section with cedar shavings (you can find them in the pet-supply section of many grocery stores). Hang them in the closet and, if necessary, around the door—just take them down if the neighbors show up! The cedar smells a lot better than mothballs."

SAFETY RECOMMENDATIONS

$ Never reuse a spray bottle. Dispose of spray bottles from cleaners or ones that have contained chemicals. New spray bottles can be purchased for a dollar or less at dollar stores.

$ Never mix ammonia with bleach, as a deadly gas is formed.

$ Never mix one type of cleaner with another, due to possible chemical reactions.

$ Keep all cleaners, even the "safe" ones, away from children and pets.

The Frugal Woman Knows...

BAKING SODA CAN BE USED FOR JUST ABOUT ANYTHING

Baking soda (or sodium bicarbonate) isn't just for keeping your refrigerator smelling fresh. It is one of the greatest all-purpose, all-natural, and nontoxic cleaning agents out there; it can be used as a first aid treatment and even serves as an ingredient in homemade beauty care preparations. Here are 20 ways one Frugal Woman has found to use the stuff in that little orange box.

1. Deodorize the refrigerator, freezer, closets, musty rooms, pet houses and bedding, cat litter boxes, and reptile or rodent cages with a bowl or sachet filled with soda.

2. In the laundry: Oil- and grease-stained clothing washes out better with soda added to the washing water. Soak and wash diapers and other laundry with baking soda for deodorizing and cleaning.

3. Polish silverware with dry soda on a damp cloth. Rub, rinse, and dry. For silver pieces without raised patterns or cemented-on handles, place the silver on aluminum foil in an enamel pot. Add boiling water and four tablespoons baking soda. Let stand, rinse, and dry.

4. To remove burned-on food from pots and pans, sprinkle soda and add one cup of water. Let soak overnight, then scrub with soda.

5. For spills in the oven or on the stovetop, immediately sprinkle soda over them and let sit. Once cooled, remove with pancake turner and scrub with dry soda on a damp sponge.

6. To remove carpet odors, sprinkle soda over carpets, leave for a couple of hours (overnight if it's not very humid), and vacuum.

7. For pet or human vomit, sprinkle the mess with soda and salt. Leave for a few hours and brush up (you do not want to use the vacuum if it's still damp).

8. Use as a paste to remove coffee or tea stains from cups.

9. Mix one cup soda and one cup cornstarch to create an underarm deodorant. Just use a powder puff or blush brush to apply after you shower. (This works especially well if your skin is sensitive to the chemicals in commercial deodorants.) You'll still perspire, but you'll have no odor.

10. To treat rashes, sunburn, diaper rash, or other skin discomforts, add a cup of soda to a warm bath and soak. To immediately treat an insect bite, make a paste of soda and water, and dab on skin.

11. For a wonderful exfoliating facial scrub, make a paste of one tablespoon soda, one tablespoon oatmeal, and some water. Remember to use gentle motions while applying.

12. Brush your teeth and gargle with soda for sweeter breath, and to help prevent gingivitis.

13. Sprinkle in shoes to replace expensive "odor-eating" powders.

14. In case of fire, always keep an extra box of baking soda by your stove for grease or electrical fire. Scatter the powder by the handful to safely put it out. Keep a container of baking soda in your garage, as well as in your car, to put out a fire. It won't damage anything it touches.

15. If a book's pages get wet, sprinkle soda over the pages, let dry, then fan the book, and brush out any remaining soda. For light mildew, the soda can be used to very gently scour the page to remove it.

16. Use as a paste to gently remove bugs and road grime from car headlights, grills, and so on.

17. In highly humid areas, moss will often grow on roofs or on outdoor carpet. Just sprinkle with soda and the moss will die, dry up, and can be swept away.

18. To remove stubborn stains from marble, Formica, or plastic kitchen surfaces, scour with a paste of baking soda and water.

19. Use baking soda to clean pencil, crayon, and black marks off walls. Mix baking soda with water to make a paste and rub over the mark until clean. An old toothbrush works wonders too.

20. Fight roaches without chemicals by leaving out a small dish of baking soda in the affected area. The soda gives the bugs gas, which they can't expel, and kills them.

The Frugal Woman Knows . . .

SALT DOES MORE THAN FLAVOR FOOD

The Romans used to pay their soldiers in salt—our word salary, *in fact, comes from* sal *(Latin for* salt*) for this very reason. And when you look at what it can do, you begin to understand why. A Frugal Woman shares her tips for using this precious substance around the house.*

1. Clean a spilled egg: If an egg breaks on the kitchen floor, sprinkle salt on the mess and leave it there for 20 minutes. The egg will congeal, so you'll be able to wipe it right up.

2. Kill grass growing in cracks in the cement or between patio stones: Sprinkle salt on the grass and pour very hot water over it. Or sprinkle coarse salt on the grass, let stand all day or overnight, then pour hot tap water over it.

3. Clean a glass coffeepot: Fill the pot with a quarter cup of table salt and a dozen ice cubes. Swish the mixture around, let sit for half an hour, fill with cold water, and rinse.

4. Halt the mountain of suds from an overflowing washing machine: Sprinkle salt on the top.

5. Clean silk and other fabric flowers: Put them in a bag of salt and shake the bag.

6. Keep windows frost-free: Dip a sponge into salt water and rub it on windows, and they won't frost up even when the mercury dips below freezing; for the same effect on your car's windshield, put salt in a little bag made of cheesecloth, moisten it slightly and rub it on.

7. Clean tarnished copper: Fill a 16-ounce spray bottle with hot white vinegar and three tablespoons of salt. Spray it onto the copper, let it sit briefly, then rub clean. (Don't do this to lacquered copper.)

8. Keep potatoes and apples from turning brown once they're sliced: Put them in salted cold water.

9. Kill poison ivy: Add three pounds of salt to a gallon of soapy water. Spray it onto leaves and stems.

10. Clean the brown spots (from starch) off a nonstick soleplate (the bottom of your iron): Sprinkle salt on a sheet of waxed paper, slide the iron across it, then rub lightly with silver polish.

11. Clean vases: Mix a third of a cup of salt and two tablespoons vinegar to form a paste. Apply to the inside of a vase (for a large vase, double or triple the quantity of paste). Let stand 20 minutes, scrub, and discard paste. Rinse vase and dry.

12. Remove wine stains: Immediately pour enough salt directly on the stain to soak up the liquid. Immerse the fabric for a half hour in cold water. Launder as usual.

13. Remove fish odors: Rub your hands with a lemon wedge dipped in salt, then rinse with water.

14. Cut rust: Remove rust from household and garden tools by using salt and a tablespoon of lemon juice. Apply the paste to the rusted area with a dry cloth and rub.

15. Give your room a breath of fresh air: Cut an orange in half, remove the pulp, and fill the peel with salt. It will provide a pleasant, aromatic scent anywhere in your home.

16. Clean a cutting board: Pour a generous amount of salt directly on the board. Rub lightly with a damp cloth. Wash in warm, sudsy water.

17. Patch small nail holes and fine cracks in plaster or wallboard: Mix two tablespoons salt, two tablespoons cornstarch, and four to five teaspoons water to make a thick, pliable paste. Fill hole, let dry, sand if necessary, and then paint.

SAVING ENERGY AND CONSERVING THE ENVIRONMENT

The Frugal Woman Knows...

SAVING MONEY AND THE ENVIRONMENT GO HAND-IN-HAND

Conserving the environment is as important to many Frugal Women as conserving money. Making their own cleaning supplies cuts down on the toxic chemicals in their homes and reduces plastic waste that would go straight into landfills. Taking measures to cut their power bills helps cut down on energy use and the drain on natural resources. All of this adds up to savings not just for themselves, but for generations to come.

As one Frugal Woman says, "I've always been frugal, but one reason why I do it has nothing to do with money—I'm an environmentalist. I think it's wrong to waste our planet's resources. When I'm thrifty, I not only help my family save money, I help save the planet as well. Now that sounds like a great deal to me!"

For a Rich Life . . .

CONSERVE THE EARTH'S RESOURCES AS WELL AS YOUR OWN

Environmentally friendly living fits very naturally (if you'll excuse the pun) into the Frugal Woman's ethos. Here is how one Frugal Woman has melded the principles of saving money and saving the earth.

Saving the earth is a whole philosophy of living, and sometimes it makes you feel like you're swimming upstream. For my family and me, it means rejecting the "buy more stuff" culture that's pushed on us by TV and other marketing. Think about how many fast-food plastic toys there are just in North America right now . . . how many bits of plastic packaging from snack foods . . . how many plastic juice boxes with plastic straws wrapped in cellophane . . . how much plastic silverware. Every one of those things costs more money than the alternatives. Here are some ways I've found to conserve money *and* the earth's resources.

Pack lunches for the kids.
Instead of eating out when I'm running errands with the kids, I bring our lunch with us. I use jelly jars for glasses for drinks-to-go, fill them with juice or milk, and screw the tops on tight.

Live like my grandmother did.
"Convenience" costs money and fills our landfills. For me, frugal, Earth-friendly living has meant quitting my job and spending a lot of time doing things the way

my grandmother did. I am aware that if we were a two-income family, we could afford a different lifestyle. But there is something about a day spent picking homegrown currants to make jam, canning tomatoes, or hanging diapers on the line that calms me.

Compost paper and kitchen waste.

We compost paper plates, napkins, and coffee filters along with our yard and kitchen waste; most food scraps go to the chickens.

Buy my kids resale and hand-me-down clothes.

These clothes look really nice too. It's amazing how many new outfits there are at garage sales with the tags still on them.

Avoid commercial television.

My kids have PBS and videos, and we make lots of trips to the library. That leaves us plenty of time for other activities. During the holiday season, we spend wonderful weeks creating cards and gifts, making wine, collecting money for charities, baking, and doing art projects.

Keep informed.

Sometimes the cheap alternative is not the best choice. Too much of the bargain stuff at chain stores is made in sweatshops or by child labor. I would rather live simply and have eggs laid today by hens whose names I know and brought in by my happy kids than work a job to buy the week-old factory-farmed ones at the store, which were probably laid by debeaked hens who spend their entire lives in a shoebox-sized cage.

Spend in ways that support my values.

I truly believe in the power of my checkbook. Every penny we spend sends ripples out into the economy and the world. I can choose which companies to support— and which not to. I like to spend my money at mom-and-pop local businesses and in ways that support the community. I am happy to support organic farmers, even if it costs a bit more.

The Frugal Woman Knows . . .

WARM UP TO ENERGY-SAVING STRATEGIES

Just turn off that light switch or change the setting on your air conditioner, and you're on your way to saving money, not to mention preserving our planet's natural resources. Here are some more measures for cutting down on sky-high energy bills.

Watch your windows.

"Keep your windows clean; this saves energy because it allows more of the sun's heat to penetrate during the winter."

——— ✦ ———

"On winter nights, keep curtains and blinds closed to prevent heat loss. Conversely, in the summer, keep shades drawn during the day to prevent the sun's heat from raising the temperature in your home."

Insulate.

"Check for air leaks around doors and windows. Adding strips of felt around them will prevent heat loss. If you don't have good windows or storm windows, use plastic to insulate."

———— ✦ ————

"If you have an attic space, make sure it's properly insulated."

———— ✦ ————

"If light switches and outlets are a source of air leaks, you can purchase special pads that go between the plates and the wall."

———— ✦ ————

"Insulate the hot water heater with a wrap."

Switch to fluorescent bulbs.

"My neighbor saved $20 on his electric bill this month and all he did was change all his incandescent bulbs to fluorescent bulbs. He said it cost him $200 to do the entire house, but it's already paying for itself."

———— ✦ ————

"Our utility company puts out a catalog that sells lighting fixtures, lightbulbs, shower heads, weatherproofing, and other energy-saving materials. They sell fluorescent bulbs at half the price the local stores do, but they only sell to their own customers. You might want to check if your electric company has a similar offer."

Reset your thermostat.

"Get a thermostat with a timer. You can save a lot on heating bills this way. Our house is divided into heating zones, so we set the heat down very low in the bedrooms during the day, when no one is in there. Then the heat goes off downstairs at night when we are upstairs sleeping. You can even set the timer to turn off the heat all day when you're out of the house, and to come on shortly before you get back home after work or school."

———— ✦ ————

"Here is what we did to save some money on our out-of-control utilities bills: We turned the thermostat down to 62 degrees during the day and 58 at night. We had some flannel sheets that we'd never used, but we soon learned how cozy they could be, combined with lots of blankets. Eventually we sold our gas logs and installed a wood stove, which we love. It will take a while to pay for itself but our gas bill is no longer $400 a month. Wood is so much cheaper. We don't use as many lights in the house now, and we stopped leaving the TV on all day. I wash the clothes in cold water and hang them out to dry on nice days instead of using the dryer."

Unplug electronics when not in use.

"Every appliance in your house that has a digital clock (VCR, microwave oven, radios, etc.) is drawing energy to keep those clocks going, even when the appliance is not in use. Do we really need to have 12 on in one house? Unplug those devices when they're not in use to cut down on your electricity bills. You can also try using battery-operated clocks and alarm clocks, and see if that saves you some money."

———— ✦ ————

"I work for a state government agency and have been doing some environmental research. I learned that appliances with remote controls use 90 (yes, 90) percent of their electricity while they are turned off. This is because they have to be 'on' in stand-by mode so they will respond when you punch the on button on the remote. So, if you just unplug your television, VCR, and stereo when they're not in use, you should see a savings in your electric bill. Try plugging all of these devices into a surge suppressor power strip. Then you can just turn the strip off, instead of unplugging so many things at once. If you want to start slowly, always remember to unplug the devices when you're on vacation or away for the weekend, or during the day when nobody is home."

Cool off with ceiling fans.

"We lowered our air conditioning bill drastically by installing ceiling fans. We found some nice ones at Wal-Mart for very reasonable prices. The savings on our electricity bills in just a few months paid for the ceiling fans."

Do cold-water washes only.

"I only wash clothes in cold water. After I started doing that, our power bills were reduced by about 30 percent!"

Cut down on dryer use.

"A guy from the power company gave me this idea—'spin' your clothes in the washer one extra time and it will cut the drying time in half. The washer takes less energy, and costs pennies for the second spin. I have been doing this and, by golly, it works! It doesn't matter if you are drying your clothes in the dryer or on the line, the less water in the clothes, the quicker they dry."

For a Rich Life...

GO OFF THE (POWER) GRID ONE WEEKEND

How much electricity do you really need to use each month? Consider going for 48 hours without any—and then see what you don't miss. One Frugal Woman shares her yearly ritual of doing just that.

Every year we have a "non-electric weekend." We do it around Earth Day as an environmental statement of sorts. We shut most things off at the fuse box, and then throw a blanket over the fridge and pretend it isn't there. I plan ahead, and make sure we'll have enough clean clothes ready. We normally use the dishwasher, but for that weekend we use the same set of plates, cups, forks, and so on, and wash them by hand after every use. Making do with so little makes me wonder why my cabinets are filled with dishes.

Rich Life Rewards:
A Frugal Woman's Tale

When my husband walked out on me for another woman my children were three and five, and I was totally unprepared mentally, emotionally, and financially to raise two children on a secretary's salary. I quickly became very creative and resourceful. We made it; they are now 19 and 22 and in college.

I love being frugal now. It stretches the imagination and keeps the mind busy. I recycle everything because I cannot stand to see anything wasted. It helps the earth, which makes me feel good. I'm a bit of an environmentalist and love the outdoors. Gardening is a hobby now; I originally took it up because I could be at home with the children. It gets me out of the house and is good exercise. I walk my dog three miles, four to five times a week for exercise; it beats getting in the car and driving to the gym, which always costs money.

When the children wanted a dog I went to the Humane Society to get him instead of buying a pedigreed dog in the pet shop window. He completed our family and has brought us so much love, laughter, and enjoyment. Now I contribute annually to the Humane Society and support that most wonderful organization. By going through the difficult times I turned my life into one which is more self-satisfying and rewarding.

—Marcia Fox, Naples, Florida

◆

CHAPTER 5

THE FRUGAL WOMAN
Decorates

I have found that by being frugal, I can be prouder of my home. Anyone can buy an upscale house and hire an interior designer and have a beautiful house. I picked out everything in my home and can remember why I bought it, restored it, or who gave it to me. When someone enters my home and compliments it, I can say thanks, because I did it all and on a very tight budget. I picked the paint color, stripped the wallpaper, made the curtains, designed *the nursery, made the bedding, repaired the Sheetrock, and hung the pictures. It was my family and friends who passed on the furniture, and painted the pictures that hang on my walls. The silver we use at our Mother's Day dinner belonged to my grandmother. That quilt in the nursery belonged to my husband and was made for him by his grandmother. The picture above the couch was drawn for me by my brother-in-law. Everything in my house has a story.*

I have taken interior design classes and have been asked by others to help design their homes. I can't. Your home tells a story about who you are, where you have been, and where you hope to go. My home tells my story. For your house to become a home, your house will have to tell yours. Maybe if the budget had been a little more flexible, I would have bought finer fabrics and had the curtains made by a professional, and perhaps I would not have to make the bed "just so" to hide the stain on the bedspread, but then I would not be able to smile all the way down to my toes when someone enters and says, "What a lovely home!"

—Kim Anderson, North Little Rock, Arkansas

———————— ◆ ————————

IF A MAN'S HOME IS HIS CASTLE, A FRUGAL WOMAN'S home is her canvas. The joys of hearth and home are important to her and, as you've heard from many Frugal Women in this book, creating a welcoming abode is something she takes great pride in. The ideas Frugal Women share over the following pages range from the simple to the extensive. If you're new to decorating, take your time and establish your style (and build your skill) as you go. One simple thing done well—whether an arrangement of treasured objects or a newly painted room—makes a grand statement.

THE FRUGAL WOMAN'S FAVORITE DECORATING SUPPLIES

Baskets

Fabric

Glue guns

Paint

Pillow stuffing

Staple gun

Sewing machine

The Frugal Woman Knows . . .

HOW TO DO IT (YOURSELF) RIGHT

Before you undertake any home project, be sure you know how to do it correctly, especially if power tools, chemicals, electrical wiring, or plumbing are involved. Having to call in a contractor to fix major mistakes—or worse, injuring yourself—is *not* frugal.

Here's how to get help—cheap—on big projects.

$ Read up on techniques in books (taken out from the library, of course) dedicated to home repair and maintenance projects.

$ Visit your local home supply store—many offer free workshops for do-it-yourself projects.

$ Ask knowledgeable friends and acquaintances for advice or help.

The Frugal Woman Knows...
WHERE TO FIND INSPIRATION ON THE CHEAP

Redesigning a whole room takes a lot of imagination—which is why so many people pay decorators to get the look they want. Use these tips to avoid that route—and still have a great-looking room in the end.

Visit the library.

"Check out the library for magazines and books. Make color photocopies of things you like—colors, styles, and furniture—and start a scrapbook. From this, start picking out the stuff you really like, and create a 'storyboard' for your room. On it put paint chips of colors you want to use, fabric samples, and pictures of the furniture. It will help you to get an overall image to work from."

Visit show homes.

"Tour new housing developments that have a show home—they are professionally decorated and are great for gathering ideas. Ask if you can take photos for reference later."

Ask about design consultations.

"Go to a large home decor/furniture store and inquire about professional decorators. These stores often have someone on staff who can do a consultation with you and help your plan—without your having to pay or buy anything."

FIVE QUICK, EASY, AND FRUGAL DECORATING TOUCHES

It should come as no surprise that Frugal Women have some wonderful ideas for low-cost, low-fuss room makeovers.

1. Put a hat on it.

"Take wicker or straw hats (maybe different sizes) and glue some flowers (dry or silk) and ribbon bows on them, leaving some plain. Hang them on nails over the top of a window, hanging into the window."

2. Use plants and pots.

"Plants are wonderful, and they add personality to any room. You can get reasonably priced ones at places like Wal-Mart. Lots of times you can get plants as gifts, or you can let others know you want plants as gifts. You can even get cheap pots and decorate them with fingernail polish; you don't need special paint. Stencils are cheap, and you can be as creative as you want."

3. Go no-sew for your windows.

"Try to find a no-sew window treatment book (I've found several at my library). There are no-sew window treatments that you can do using glue, staples, and so on."

4. Use a natural touch.

"For the earthy sort, nature provides all kinds of freebies to decorate with. Try an interesting branch hung behind the sofa, driftwood or shells from the beach arranged as wall art, dried grasses in an old pot, a stack of pinecones on a shelf, river stones used as paperweights, and feathers used as bookmarks."

5. Make your own rock fountain.

"Go out and collect a few flat stones. Go to your local hardware store and buy a large stone bowl (garden section) with a two-inch-high rim. Buy an inexpensive garden pump (the smallest you can find) and a foot of clear tubing. Then put together a rock fountain. It is fun and relatively cheap."

FRUGAL IN THE CITY: QUICK APARTMENT FIXES

Decorating a rented space can seem tough—besides a possibly limited budget or not wanting to dump money into a short-term space, the landlord may not allow you to undertake a painting job or may limit your color choice to white, white, or white. But your home should feel like home—here are a few quick ways to warm up even the most spartan of spaces and give personality to your dwelling.

$ Start by buying some houseplants and candles. They are relatively inexpensive and can add coziness to your apartment.

$ Baskets are always wonderful, and usually very affordable. Hang them on the walls to cover unsightly cracks, unused phone jacks, or other eyesores.

$ If you have the bare-wall apartment blues, add texture by hanging a quilt or an arrangement of old china plates.

For a Rich Life . . .

ACQUIRE INSTANT ART

A limited budget needn't consign you to barren walls. Here are some Frugal Women's ways to create gallery-worthy displays at home—without having to win the lottery.

$ Many discount stores, such as Sam's Club, World Market, Meijer, and Wal-Mart, have inexpensive artwork that you can add to your walls.

$ Calendars often have cool pictures; cut the pictures out and frame them with cheap frames or cardboard covered in contact paper.

$ Are you an animal lover? Frame wildlife and nature pictures from magazines such as *National Geographic* and display throughout your room.

$ Cover an unsightly wall with family photos: Buy inexpensive matching frames at a discount or dollar store, and arrange a display of your favorite portraits. If you have a scanner, scan them in and then print them all at one size (8x10, for instance), to give the wall a more uniform look.

$ Display best-loved pieces of your children's artwork in simple, inexpensive frames—arranged elegantly, they can give your room an eclectic, "country primitive" look.

The Frugal Woman Knows...
WINNING WALL IDEAS

One way to overcome plain walls is to apply decorative painting techniques, ranging from simple stencils and sponging to more advanced *trompe d'oeil* effects. But if time (along with money) is in short supply or you have your heart set on a wallpaper look, try one of these frugal ideas.

$ Use contact paper instead of wallpaper (not only is it cheaper, it's easier to hang as well!).

$ Cover your walls with sheets of themed papers meaningful to you. One Frugal Woman pasted sheet music on her walls and decorated with musical instruments. You could do this with maps, illustrated vintage magazine covers (perhaps found at a flea market or garage sale), or whatever reflects your passions.

$ Tack floor-to-ceiling fabrics to your walls—this is especially good if you live in rented space, where you may not want to (or be allowed to) invest in more permanent wall decor.

MAKE YOUR OWN THROW PILLOWS

Look in any decorating magazine and you'll see that throw pillows are a classic way to add a splash of color or a special accent to a room. Frugal Women have come up with some clever and innovative ways to turn inexpensive materials into eye-catching throw pillows.

Convert some place mats.
"I had seen some beautiful Asian-style, silk throw pillows but they wanted $85 each. I knew I could make them myself, but I couldn't find the right type of silk. Then I found some place mats on sale that were almost identical to the pillows. I bought four for less than $5. When I got home, I discovered that each place mat was already two pieces sewn together. I opened up a seam and filled them with some stuffing. The place mats even had a decorative bead detail in the corners."

Sew together bandannas.
"Since my great room has a Southwestern design theme, I purchased several bandannas. They are the perfect size for the ready-made pillow forms. I took two bandannas and sewed them together, leaving a space wide enough to insert the pillow filler, and then hand-sewed the opening closed. Depending on what style you have, you might even find some inexpensive scarves that you can do the same thing with."

Save those old curtains.
"Replacing some stained or worn curtains? If they still match your overall décor, don't throw them away. Even if they are stained, there might be enough clean fabric left to sew some pillows."

USE BEDSHEETS FOR MORE THAN JUST SLEEPING

Fabric, like fresh paint, is a quick-and-easy way to give a room new life. Try using old bedsheets (or new ones that you find at a white sale) for these decorating projects.

Curtains

The broad hem across the top of a flat sheet is big enough to thread a curtain rod through and hang over a window. Or drape over a tension rod and hang in an open doorway, built-in shelves, or an exposed closet.

Duvet Covers

Sew three sides of a bedsheet together; add some buttonholes and buttons, or snaps. Voila!

Tablecloths

Drape over an accent table as is, letting it sweep to the floor. Or cut to the size of your table and hem.

Canopies for Four-Poster Beds

Drape the sheet over the posts of your bed (you might have to add ribbon to keep it tied to the posts). Though it won't fall to the floor, it will make a nice short canopy. Depending on the size of the sheet and your bed, you may have to get two sheets and sew them together.

Wall Coverings

Cut off the hems and soak the sheet in liquid starch. Smooth it onto a wall that you want to cover up. You have instant wallpaper! When you move or get tired of it just rip it off, leaving the original wall finish undisturbed.

Lampshades

Get an extra flat sheet that matches your new duvet cover, and re-cover your bedside lampshades for an elegant, put-together look. (See page 121 for detailed instructions.)

Seat Cushions

Cut the sheet to fit over seat cushions, stitch to close, and use for your wooden kitchen chairs.

The Frugal Woman Knows...

HOW TO GET CUSTOM PAINT FOR CHEAP

Think you have to spend big bucks to get gorgeous designer colors for your wall paint? Think again—here's how one Frugal Woman turns other's indecision into her gain.

I have been buying the "oops" paint from Lowe's and Home Depot. They have such good return policies that there are usually several shelves of "oops" paint. Nothing wrong with it, it was just the "wrong" color or someone bought too much. I have spent about $40 total on paint for most of the rooms in my house. My best find so far was Ralph Lauren Suede (chocolate brown) paint for $5 a gallon—usually $30 per gallon. The trick is to check the "oops" section often, and be a bit flexible with color.

TAKE SLIPCOVERS FROM SHABBY TO CHIC

One Frugal Woman tells how to use tea bags for a low-cost couch makeover.

If you have slipcovers for your couch that have become badly stained, here's a frugal solution. For the cost of a large box of tea bags, you can try tea-dyeing them—and you'll end up with a beautiful light brown color. It should work with any light fabric; I have done it with white pillow shams for my antique bed. Wash and dry the slipcover before you get started. Then boil a large amount of water in your biggest pot and throw in a box of tea bags. You can start with just 20 tea bags and test a piece of scrap material for 10 minutes. If you want it darker, add more tea bags. Let the tea cool a little and transfer it to a large tub, along with the slipcover, and let it sit for as long as you want. The longer you wait, the darker the color. Finally, run the slipcover through the rinse cycle in your washer.

The Frugal Woman Knows...

HOW TO TEACH AN OLD ROOM NEW TRICKS

We'll say it again: Living frugally doesn't mean giving up style in order to net savings. If you've consigned yourself to living with a decor you can't abide because of the presumed cost of an overhaul, think again. Frugal Women have come up with these inspired, cheap-and-easy decorating methods to solve just about any "this old room" issue.

Make a small room look larger.

Have a space that feels small and cramped? You don't need to break out a wall to give it a more expansive feel. Try some of these cheap-and-easy decorating ideas for doing just that.

———— ◆ ————

"Paint the walls a light, neutral color and add touches of your favorite colors through accessories such as throw pillows. If you really love darker-colored walls (because they are so cozy, of course), you will have to expand the room visually in other ways such as a large mirror on the wall, plenty of lamps, or uplights to throw light up the walls and onto the ceiling."

———— ◆ ————

"Whatever color you choose for your walls, paint the ceiling two shades lighter, and paint the trim in an even lighter shade."

———— ◆ ————

"Keep the paint scheme monochromatic (different shades of the same color). For example, if you paint the walls a dark color and the trim white, it will make the room look more 'cut up' and less spacious."

———— ✦ ————

"Try putting a narrow wallpaper border along the walls where they meet the ceiling, with a background color lighter than the walls, that matches the ceiling color—it will help 'raise' a low ceiling."

———— ✦ ————

"Use several different forms of lighting, rather than one large overhead light. Track lighting can come in inexpensive forms (try bargain stores or garage sales). If you focus the lighting on an opposing side of the room, say on a picture, it draws the eye across the room, rather than up at a low ceiling. Lamps also help soften a room and create depth."

———— ✦ ————

"Use drapes to create a 'faux' window, or make a window look larger than it actually is. Just buy rods and drapes that are wider than the window and curtains that are heavy enough so that you cannot see through them. But try to get the drapes in a light color, so that the room stays bright and appears larger."

Update old wood paneling.

Is your frugally bought fixer-upper plagued with 1970s paneling? Try one of these ideas to modernize the room without going through the expense of tearing it all out and replacing the wallboard.

"With the grooves in paneling, it is easy to stripe the walls. Choose two coordinating colors of paint, and alternate the shades on each panel around the room."

———— ✦ ————

"To get a summery Cape Cod look, paint the walls a pale blue or green, then cover that with a coat of fresh white, and sandpaper the top layer off lightly to make it look worn and faded."

———— ✦ ————

"You have a few choices with paneling. You can prime the paneling, then paint over—a very cheap option. Or you can spackle the spaces (vertical lines), then spray-spackle the entire board, prime, and then paint. That second option might cost a little more, but you'll save a lot of money if you do the work yourself. And it looks exactly like brand-new Sheetrock when you're done."

Refresh tired kitchen cabinets.

Updating your kitchen doesn't take thousands of dollars of new cabinetry and countertops. A weekend or two of work may be all you need to give your room a fresh look.

"We painted our dark 1970s kitchen cabinets a fresh white. It was a lot of work, but it looks wonderful. We used a product called TSP (tri-sodium phosphate). It takes the varnish off and gives you a base you can prime and paint."

———— ✦ ————

"Our cabinets had a raised stenciled design on them which we had to remove before we could repaint them a lighter color. We sanded down the designs and then put on a coat of primer paint before we painted. You can cover about anything with Kilz primer—I used it when we wanted to paint our bathroom white, over the old brownish-red color. It worked great."

———— ✦ ————

"There are primers that will stick to any surface. Before you repaint your cabinets, try the one by Benjamin Moore called Fresh Start."

———— ✦ ————

"Here's an idea if you're on a really tight budget. Tear paper sacks (the thinner ones) into large pieces so the edges will be jagged. Wad them into a ball to crumple, then smooth out and paint. Apply them to cabinets like wallpaper, then finish with polyurethane. This will cover anything unsightly. Try it on one door first, to see if you will like it."

———— ✦ ————

"Decoupage is a great way to cover ugly cabinets. I've heard of people using things like old maps or sheet music. I could see some antique maps looking great for the doors."

———— ✦ ————

"If your cabinets have wood trim on the door itself, like mine, then this will work. I am taking down all of the doors and putting on TSP—it strips the gloss and the grease and anything else gross off of the wood. I am then cutting out the inner fake-wood part, leaving just the frame, and installing glass. I bought plain glass and sprayed it with glass froster (comes in a spray can)—this is much cheaper than buying frosted glass. You can paint the frame part if you like."

Apply a theme.

Love those elegantly themed rooms you see in decorating books and magazines? You can put together your own look for a pittance with some supplies from the craft or dollar store. Here are ideas from several Frugal Women on creating a cheery sunflower theme for a kitchen; you can apply the principles to any other theme you want to use in your room.

"Update your curtains/window treatments—if you can sew, you can do this very cheaply. Check your local fabric store for prints with sunflowers (or whatever theme you're looking for)."

———— ✦ ————

"Prints—check out discount stores and flea markets, for good bargains on prints and frames."

———— ✦ ————

"Decorate a grapevine wreath or swag with silk flowers to hang on the wall or over a doorway."

———— ✦ ————

"Buy a plastic or silk greenery garland, and some silk or plastic flowers. Use a glue gun to attach the flowers to the garland, and drape the finished garland on the top of a china closet or hutch."

———— ✦ ————

"If you can put up those little wooden ledge shelves or wire rack shelves, you could find some knickknacks to display. Try flea markets and yard sales."

———— ✦ ————

"If you have a glass-fronted china closet or cabinets, keep your eyes peeled for serving pieces with your theme that you could display."

———— ✦ ————

"Stencil some sunflowers around a window or door as a border, maybe just a few here and there for whimsical effect."

———— ✦ ————

"Do you have an old bench or other piece of furniture in the room? You could paint it a cheery color and decoupage sunflowers on it—cut them out from wallpaper or wrapping paper."

———— ✦ ————

"Keep an eye out for sales on decorative accessories such as canisters, kitchen towels, magnets, and spoon rests."

ONE PERSON'S TRASH IS ANOTHER'S TREASURE

Forget about hitting the mall when you need something new—a little dedicated "trash picking" can get you everything from mint-condition furniture to building supplies for a pittance—or even free. In addition to regularly scoping out garage sales, flea markets, Goodwill, the Salvation Army, and thrift stores, here are some venues Frugal Women count as best bets.

Clean up on clean-up days.

"A lot of towns have an annual clean-up day, when people can set out the stuff that can't be put out on a regular trash day—you can find a lot of furniture, building supplies and more!"

Go where the movers are.

"Drive around apartment complexes, especially at the end of the month when people are moving out. I've gotten a bamboo chair, ottoman, fireplace screen, and an entire outdoor bamboo set with a glass table and four chairs!"

Check out student specials.

"College dorms at the end of the semester are another great place to check out. You won't believe what those kids throw away."

Build your relationship with builders.

"Some of my really big finds come from the used builder's supply store. Look under 'Building Materials' in the Yellow Pages. There will usually be a couple that call themselves discount stores. Call and ask if they have a secondhand supply section. This stuff is usually really cheap. Also, look under 'Demolition.' Most of the ones in my Yellow Pages say they sell used lumber, brick, doors, and windows. Also, don't be shy about stopping to pick up materials from the trash on the street by a house that's being remodeled or rebuilt. The owners usually don't mind, and the trash folks would thank you for saving them a few minutes, if they could."

How to Assess a "Free" Find

When presented with the seemingly perfect curbside or Dumpster find, ask yourself the following:

1. Is it free for me to take?

2. Can I fit it in the car?

3. If the condition isn't perfect, can I fix it?

4. If I can't repair it, are there parts that can be salvaged and reused?

5. Do I have room for it in my house?

The Frugal Woman Knows...

HOW TO GIVE NEW LIFE TO OLD

Is your basement or garage full of found items that you don't know what to do with? Do you haunt flea markets thinking, *That's gorgeous, but what would I do with it?* Well, you're not alone. Frugal Women are brimming full of creative makeover ideas for everything from old wooden doors to breadboxes—use these as inspiration for your own projects!

Dressers

Turn the old bureau you found into kitchen or craft-room workspace with one of the following methods.

"Tile the top of it: Buy some cheap black and white tiles, or choose another color that fits your kitchen decor."

———— ✦ ————

"Laminate the top of it: You can get the glue-on type laminate at any home store, and you can probably find some to match your existing countertops."

———— ✦ ————

"Get a piece of plywood cut to size, sand the top yourself, and turn the top into a huge cutting board. To make it prettier, you could mark out a few inches of border and stencil or decoupage, and then shellac the border."

———— ✦ ————

"Cut fiberglass (you can get it at any hardware store) to fit the top. Attach it to the dresser with Fun-Tak so that it won't slide around—yet can be easily removed if you decide that you want to use it as a dresser again."

———— ✦ ————

"Get some melamine-laminated chipboard; the hardware store will probably cut it to size for free. For a few dollars more, you can add pretty molding, which you can glue on to the unfinished edges and paint yourself."

Dresser Drawers

Have (or found) a dresser where the frame is beyond repair, but with drawers still in usable condition? Try these ideas.

"Use old drawers as planting boxes. Use as-is, or give them a shabby-chic, distressed look. Drill a few holes in the bottom and add rocks or packing peanuts for drainage. Add soil, then add your plants, and you're done. Works with virtually any size drawer."

———— ✦ ————

"Use spare drawers for extra storage under the bed. Just slide them in with the handle facing out. It's cheap, easy, and can give you much-needed extra places to tuck things away. You could even put the drawer on wheels to make it easier to slide in and out from under your bed."

Chairs

Scooped up a mismatched set of wooden chairs at the flea market, or were bequeathed some by a friend who is upgrading her kitchen? Give them a fresh look with these ideas.

"Paint and stencil them to match. Also, maybe make little tie-on cushions for them. But check to make sure they aren't worth more left alone: I refinished an old desk once, and then found out that I'd knocked nearly $200 off its value."

———— ✦ ————

"Paint them all a matching color. After they've dried, sand off the paint in spots for a vintage, worn look. Then make or purchase cushions to match your curtains or tablecloth!"

———— ✦ ————

"Make chair 'throws.' They are rather simple to make, and they really tie the chairs together. It's a piece of fabric that covers the chair back like a pillowcase (slips over the back). You can tie them at the bottom."

End Tables

End (or side) tables are the perfect size to reinvent as a footrest or ottoman. This little overhaul requires almost no skills beyond the ability to use a stapler and glue gun.

"I 'rescued' an old rattan end table without a top. So I found a piece of plywood and my husband cut it to fit. (The lumberyard or hardware store can do this for you too.) When I was washing some pillows, I noticed one just about matched the size of my plywood. I placed it on the plywood, added some quilt backing for good measure, stapled pretty fabric over the whole thing, glued it all onto the rattan table, and voila, I had a new ottoman. It's gorgeous and didn't cost a dime."

Filing Cabinets

Filing cabinets can be used to store almost anything in your home, not just papers. So don't turn one down just because you don't have a home office. Here are some ideas for taking their look from office-functional to family-room-friendly.

"Ask an expert at the paint store to recommend a good primer before you get started, and paint to match your room."

——— ◆ ———

"Cover scratches or dents by gluing cutouts of wallpaper over them. (For instance, if you wanted a travel theme in your room, use cutouts of airplanes or boats.) Or decoupage the sides with paper of your choice."

——— ◆ ———

"Turn a two-drawer file cabinet into a table: Cut a circle out of plywood, place that over the file cabinet, cover it with a tablecloth (and even a glass top if you're ambitious), and you have a table with a filing cabinet underneath. Place a lamp or pictures on top and you have an attractive, decorative area."

Kitchen and Cooking Implements

Old bowls, pans, and pots may have outlived their usefulness for food preparation, but not as home decoration.

"Use old, stained or cracked wooden bowls to hold such things as reading material, dried flower bouquets, or hand towels. Or leave it near the door for dropping things in, like mail and keys."

———— ✦ ————

"Use discarded iron skillets as decorative elements: For small skillets, set a pillar candle in the center and surround with potpourri. For a medium or large-sized skillet, group several candles in it, surround them with potpourri or gourds, and use as a centerpiece."

Hutches

Don't be afraid to take a find apart to suit your personal style.

"I found a hutch for my dining room. It was a quite a bit of work but a labor of love all the same. It had glass doors on the top half—not nice ones, but really cheap, dated-looking ones. I removed the doors, painted the exterior of the hutch a grayish color, and the entire interior an ocean-green color. It will be great for displaying my collection of eclectic dishes on the top. I'll use the enclosed bottom half for storing my overflowing kitchen tools."

Ladders

Use old ladders too rickety to support a person for light-weight, country-inspired displays.

"I recently found two ladders in the trash. The five-foot ladder is now in my dining room to hang some plants. The smaller, free-standing ladder is in my living room—I hung some decorating magazines from the rungs."

Lamps

Salvage a working lamp with a destroyed or ugly shade by making your own.

"Roll the existing lampshade on some brown paper, and use a pencil to trace the lampshade as you roll it. Cut out the template that you have just made and use it as a pattern to make a new cover for your shade out of some pretty fabric."

Lattice

Even if you don't have a garden, sections of old lattice can be a real decorating find!

"Give your room a garden feel by hanging the lattice from an interior wall, and stencil a flowering vine over the lattice to complete the look."

——— ✦ ———

"Weave Christmas lights and silk flowers through it and suspend from your ceiling or hang on a wall."

——— ✦ ———

"Attach it to a closet wall, or on the inside of a closet door, and use it to hang handbags, belts, or other items that would otherwise end up in a jumbled mess on your closet floor. Small sections of lattice can be used in your bathroom or bedroom to hang hair accessories or necklaces."

Lazy Susans

Those hallmarks of 1970s family-style eating can be reused for many things—here are just a few.

"Paint it to look like faux marble and use it as a candle holder in the middle of a table."

———— ✦ ————

"Use it as a plant stand near a window, taller plants in the center and smaller plants around the outside. Turn it to let all the plants get enough light; you'll also be able to water your plants more easily."

———— ✦ ————

"Varnish it and use it for playing board games—just spin it around for each person's turn."

———— ✦ ————

"Remove the spinning base and use the circular top to make a sundial for the garden."

Shutters

Bring old shutters indoors for a charming antiques display system.

"Tall, old wooden shutters make a great way to display antique kitchen utensils. Just attach wires through the shutters to mount them to the wall, then hang utensils from hooks on the shutter slats. It looks great in the kitchen or dining room. You can also use it to keep new kitchen utensils handy if your drawers are overcrowded."

Table Tops

A good wooden-topped table—even without legs—can be given new life as stunning wall art.

"My sister was moving and her table broke. She was going to toss it, so I got it instead. All I could see was the solid top, begging me to paint it! I sanded it and painted faux seed packets on it, along with a few vegetables such as tomatoes, carrots, and asparagus. Then I put a glaze over the top to age it a bit and hung it on my kitchen wall. I get a lot of compliments on it. I used leftover paint, so the only thing I paid for was the glaze."

Wooden Doors

Don't close your mind to the possibilities an old door opens for your home.

"Create a worktable out of an old door by setting it on two sturdy sawhorses, and use it to do painting projects, woodworking, or potting plants."

——— ✦ ———

"Create a rustic desk by placing a door atop two file cabinets."

——— ✦ ———

"Use it as a pot rack in your kitchen: Paint it to go with your kitchen, Then add large eye hooks to each corner, and set four hooks into your ceiling spaced to match the corners of the door. (Try to set the ceiling hooks into the studs for greatest stability.) Suspend the door using several inches of chain (more if you have high ceilings) attached on one end to the hooks in the ceiling and on the other to the hooks on the door. Attach hardware for hanging your pots and pans, and use the top of the door to display your pretty collectibles."

——— ✦ ———

"Make a bench or window seat by just adding some store-bought legs and some throw pillows."

——— ✦ ———

"If you've found several doors, turn them into a folding screen by hinging them together. Paint, stencil, or decoupage them to match your décor, and hang family pictures or the children's artwork as a finishing touch."

Window Frames

Many owners of old homes toss single-paned, wooden-framed windows in favor of newer, more energy-efficient versions. Keep your eyes open if old houses are being renovated near you. Here are some clever uses for discarded windows.

"Use windows as armoire doors. Attach them with hinges to an old bookshelf or open cabinet, and you've got a glass-fronted display case!"

——— ✦ ———

"Remove the glass panes, replace them with mirror glass, and hang it on the wall for a country-style mirror."

———— ✦ ————

"Create a wall hanging by spray-painting the frames, then gluing on seashells and wild flowers."

10 Things a "Trash Hunter" Needs on Hand for Renovations

1. Paint

2. Paint thinner

3. Sandpaper

4. Soap and water

5. Glue

6. Idea book

7. Creativity

8. Elbow grease

9. Intuition—don't hesitate. If you like it, do it.

10. Pride—enjoy your work. Put items on display for everyone to see.

The Frugal Woman Knows...

IF IT'S "TOO PRETTY TO THROW AWAY," DON'T

Buying fancy papers and fabrics for projects can add up. The Frugal Woman's secret: Hang on to paper odds and ends as you find them. Keeping these materials on hand allows you the chance to indulge your creativity on the fly (and without having to pay an arm and a leg at the craft store). Stuff to save for decoupage and other projects:

$ Calendar pages

$ Good-quality wrapping paper

$ Greeting cards

$ Magazine covers

$ Maps

$ Newspaper (especially the comics pages)

$ Seed packets

$ Wallpaper scraps

The Frugal Woman Knows...

HOW TO REUSE JUST ABOUT ANYTHING

Before you toss your old stuff, no matter how "junky" it is, give it one more pass to see how you might reuse it in your home. Remember: Besides saving you money, every item you don't throw away is one less piece of trash that ends up in a landfill. As one Frugal Woman relates, "Before I ever throw out a box, a can, or even broken parts to things, I study them to think where I could possibly use them in my home. Small boxes cut in half and covered with contact paper become instant (free) drawer organizers. Cans are transformed into nail or pencil containers. A broken lampshade helped me make a Halloween costume. Never underestimate 'junk.' It might be exactly what you were looking for."

Be sure to designate some space for saving your "junk." One Frugal Woman tells of the space in which she stores her treasures: "I call it my craft closet—my husband cringes when I ask him to get anything out of it. I have a shelf of cardboard tubes from toilet paper, paper towels, and aluminum foil; one for baby food jars; one for detergent boxes, and so on. Whenever something breaks in the house, he knows that I have the parts and the skills to repair it. And he's always happy when he doesn't have to spend money on something new."

Now, for how to use the stuff you've saved . . .

Calendars

As the old year passes, save calendar artwork for new uses. Here are a few ideas.

$ Use the pictures to decoupage everything from plant stands to boxes to tables.

$ Tear out pictures and frame them (frames made for record albums work well). For instance, you could use pages from a cartoon character calendar to give a child's room a theme quickly and cheaply.

$ Cut up the pictures and use them in personalized, oversized Valentine's Day cards. Calendars with cute pictures of animals are especially good. You can make this a family project—kids love it.

Cans

Recycling laws have made us all more aware of what we do with metal cans after we've emptied them. But here are some ways to recycle these common trash items in your home.

$ Use cans as planters for your garden: You can paint or decorate them in a variety of ways; punch a hole in the bottom for drainage.

$ Make a lantern by punching holes in a metal can using a sharp nail. You can create your own design or follow a stencil. Set a candle inside when finished.

$ Use in storage bins to scoop out pet food, soil, fertilizer, and so on.

$ Attach four large, thick-sided cans (such as those from paint or stain) to the bottom of a board using screws or bolts, which will elevate the board enough to make a step stool or a sitting stool for those odd jobs at funny heights—in the garden or fiddling with a bicycle.

$ Glue or screw cans of varying heights onto a long board, and use as an organizer of pencils, pens, scissors, ruler, makeup brushes, combs, and other tall stuff.

$ Use soup cans as biscuit cutters.

Carpeting

Use carpet remnants—or the stuff you just tore out of a room—to

$ Build a scratching post for your favorite feline.

$ Cut pieces to fit the rungs of a ladder for a no-slip surface.

$ Line the floor of your doghouse. (Just tack it down so the dog doesn't pull it out.) Or line a box with it to create a cozy bed for your cat.

Chicken Wire

Small sections of chicken wire (left over, perhaps, from fencing in a vegetable garden) can be used in a variety of ways.

$ Put it in a frame and add hooks to hang kitchen utensils, or pin herbs to it to hang them dry.

$ Use it to protect bulbs (such as tulips, garlic, or shallots) the squirrels often dig up. Lay over your bulb bed and cover with mulch; the shoots will come up through the holes. When it's time to dig up your bulbs, cut off the tops, brush off the mulch, pull up the chicken wire, and remove the bulbs.

$ Staple it to your garden fence and use it as a trellis for a quick-growing flowering vine, such as morning glories.

Clothing

Outgrown clothing in good condition, of course, should be handed on to another Frugal Woman or resold at a thrift store. But for those pieces stained or torn beyond repair, try the following.

$ Turn flannel shirts and jeans into quilted throws for your family room by cutting them into squares and patching them together into two large "sheets." Sandwich quilt backing between the two panels and sew together.

$ Make an heirloom quilt with sections of your child's prettiest baby clothes.

$ Use wash-softened T-shirts as rags for cleaning and dusting, washing your car, or applying wood stain.

REUSE, RECYCLE—AND GET ORGANIZED?

How do you combine the Frugal Woman's principles of paring down your stuff *and* reusing what you've got as much as possible? Here are a few simple guidelines to follow.

Understand the point of paring down.

Living a simpler life is not about enduring an austere existence. It's about excising the stuff you don't need from your life and environment. If you need something (or think you will in the future), then there's no point in getting rid of it—you'll just have to run to the store for a new one.

Save only what you really believe you can find a use for.

If you're not a quilter (and have no intention of becoming one), hanging on to old clothes or fabric scraps may not be the most logical path. If you despise crafts, saving paper for decoupage is a waste of space and effort. But if you're an avid gardener, stray pieces of twine, old panty hose, and chicken wire—all useful for creating plant supports—may be just the things worth making space for.

Be organized about what you save.

Designate a closet or shelving area to keep your "I may need this" treasures, and group like items together within this area so you can find them quickly and easily when necessity calls.

Regularly review what you're saving.

If you have two laundry baskets full of paper towel tubes, for instance, and haven't so much as pulled one out in six months, it may be time to stop collecting them. The three dressers you "rescued" from a curbside hunt last year and still haven't gotten around to refinishing may belong on your own curb during the next town pickup. Set a time limit for keeping junk (especially big junk), and if you haven't used your stores by then, toss it.

Give what you don't need to someone who does.

Remembering that one woman's trash is another's treasure, check around before you send your "good" junk to the dump. Armloads of paper-towel rolls, boxes of stray buttons, and heaps of cardboard are frequently in demand by preschools and kindergartens. The woman down the street may be an avid quilt maker, and love the old floral dresses you're tossing.

Costume Jewelry

Earrings missing their mates, broken bead necklaces, and even items too garish to wear can be turned into a host of projects.

$ Use stud earrings to dress up pillar candles. Just press them into the wax in a random design. Once the wax melts down to them, just pull out the earrings and put them aside for your next project.

$ Attach old pins to throw pillows, or use as tiebacks for drapes.

$ Use the beads from a broken strand of fake pearls to embellish craft projects.

$ Dangly earrings can be put through the fabric on curtains to jazz them up, or detached from their posts or hooks and attached to a chain—these make great charm bracelets, especially for little girls.

$ For gaudy, unusable jewelry, get a medium-sized wooden box and paint it like a pirate's treasure chest. Put all your hideous jewelry inside and bury it for a little boy—he won't care how ugly it is. It's treasure!

Curtain Panels

If you're replacing or have found panel curtains, give them new life—even if stained—by using sections to create

$ Kitchen café curtains

$ Slipcovers for chairs

$ Throw pillows

Fabric

Just about any collection of odds and ends can be used to make patchwork quilts, pillows, napkins, and place mats. Here are a few other ideas for using up remnants of cloth.

$ Stitch small pieces into bags and fill with potpourri for sachets.

$ Heavy fabric (such as canvas or denim) can be used to make aprons with big pockets for garden tools, clothespins, or cooking tools.

$ If you have some fabric with a large floral print, cut out the flowers and use them to appliqué an apron for special occasions.

$ Cut and stitch fabric pieces into doll clothes.

Grocery Bags

If you use store-supplied bags to carry home your groceries, you can

$ Line household wastebaskets with plastic bags.

$ Use paper bags for any craft project calling for brown paper, or cut into sheets for children's doodle pads.

Milk Crates

These all-purpose metal and plastic bins aren't just for holding milk cartons!

$ Stack several together to use as a bookcase, storage for children's toys, or as supports under a board for a desk or work space.

$ Use under the sink for holding cleaning supplies, or attach to the wall in your laundry room to store detergents.

$ Cover with fabric, flip upside down, and use as a footstool.

Pillowcases

Somehow, long after the rest of a sheet set has gone to its grave, the pillowcases are left moldering in your linen closet. Put them to use by

$ Turning them into art or garden smocks for toddlers—just cut holes for their arms and heads.

$ Creating drawstring bags—slit small holes in the hem and slide string, ribbon, or rope through it and tie. Perfect for holding kids' toys, taking to the beach, or storing dirty clothes.

$ Decorating solid-colored cases with fabric paint and using to wrap gifts.

Sheet Metal

Have extra material from a home renovation project (or found some discarded after your neighbors finished theirs)? Try one of these projects.

$ Make your own outdoor candle holders by punching designs into the sheet metal using a hammer and strong nail, rolling the metal into a cylinder and setting on a saucer.

$ Make a colonial-style lampshade: Buy a cheap paper lampshade (or use one you already have), and remove the shade part. Trace the shape onto the sheet metal. Punch holes into sheet metal using a hammer and heavy nail. Cut out metal to shape of the shade, using traced lines as a guide. Affix to shade frame by crimping sheet metal around the wire frame.

$ Give a glass-paned cupboard door a country look by replacing the glass panes with punched metal squares.

$ Make garden tags by cutting the metal into small rectangles and attaching them to wooden or metal stakes.

$ Cut into squares, emboss the squares, and use as ceiling tiles.

Shoeboxes

Use shoeboxes to store and organize such items as sewing patterns, ribbons, trims, and buttons in your sewing room; flower seeds in your garage; notepads, paper clips, and pushpins on your desk; candles in a kitchen drawer; acrylic paint bottles in your craft room. Here are some more ideas.

$ Make a small storage chest. Take nine large boxes, all of them the same size. Remove one short end from each. Attach them together to form a cube. Then slide a smaller shoebox into each of the cube's openings for drawers. Use wire and beads for the drawer pulls.

$ Cover them with colored paper to make treasure boxes for young children.

$ Decoupage them with maps of the places you've traveled to and use them to store vacation and travel memorabilia.

Tea Tins

If one of your personal indulgences happens to be high-quality tea packaged in lovely tins, give those metal boxes a second life with these ideas.

$ Decorate or leave "as is" to store items such as buttons, coins, dental floss, dice and game pieces, jewelry, makeup, nail clippers, paperclips, sewing supplies, stamps, thumbtacks, or just about anything else you can think of.

$ Spray-paint them with pretty colors, put sand in them, then put them outside to be used as ashtrays for visiting smokers. The lid prevents the ashes from blowing away and making a mess.

Wooden Crates and Boxes

Don't spend money on catchall boxes from an organizing store if you've already got the basics on hand.

$ Attach fabric to the inside with thumbtacks, and use in your living room to store CDs, videos, and a few books, or to stash your TV remote.

$ Hang on the wall for use as a shelf.

$ In the bathroom, set smaller crates or boxes on the top of the toilet to hold bath sponges, soaps, and a couple of magazines.

$ In the kitchen, use to store cookie cutters, kitchen linens, or spice jars.

$ Use as an inbox at your computer to organize bills.

$ Fill with scrap paper and art supplies for your kids.

Wallpaper

Wallpaper remnants can be put to many uses—nowhere near a wall!

$ Cut out elements of the pattern and use to decoupage furniture, boxes, or whatever strikes your fancy.

$ Use vinyl wallpaper to cover old or stained plastic patio furniture. It scrubs off just as well as a vinyl tablecloth—and you won't worry about the kids or dog pulling it off!

$ Cover your journal or the kids' schoolbooks with it.

$ Use some to cover a lampshade.

$ Create a cute message board by laying pieces of old wallpaper (maybe with a patchwork or checkered pattern) over corkboard. You can replace the wallpaper when it gets full of holes.

RICH LIFE REWARDS:
A FRUGAL WOMAN'S TALE

My rental townhouse had last been decorated in the 1970s. It was in a historic district, designed by a woman in the 1920s, and just adorable. I wanted a cottage look, but I was just barely getting on my financial feet. (I felt proud when I was able to pay the phone and electric bills in the same week!) So I was shocked by the $80 price for a roll of plain-old yellow-and-white-striped wallpaper. At that rate, my dining room would cost about $360.

This is what my place looks like: The living room has yellow polished apple balloon shades with pink cabbage roses and small light blue flowers, under blue-and-white striped swag drapes, which I made. The furniture includes a vintage 1940s sofa and club chair that I picked up at a yard sale for $85 and upholstered in navy blue damask. Since the living room was large and less than cozy, I installed floor-to-ceiling shelves that wrapped around an odd corner and filled them with baskets, birdhouses, books, ivy, antique toys and floral prints. It was a very warm, inviting room, with a dull dining room backdrop.

Here's what I had to work with: white walls, a picture window, a stark square opening from the living room, and a harsh 1970s wire light fixture with a big white bulb glaring out. And no budget. Here are my frugal solutions.

Faux Wallpaper

Rather than coughing up $360 for the wallpaper, I got out my level and taped off my own stripes, which I then painted with $15 worth of yellow paint.

Window and Light Fixture Treatments

To deal with the window, I sewed balloon shades identical to those in the living room and fronted them with pink ticking-striped, tab-topped curtains. I wove two yards of pink gingham cloth in and out of the wire frame of that wretched light fixture, softening the whole look and offering a pink glow to the whole room.

Living Room Entrance

For the sharp opening to the living room, I looked at fretwork, to the tune of $600. I couldn't afford that. Instead, I soaked a $4 wreath in hot water, snipped the vine holding it together, unfurled it to fit the opening and nailed it in place. To this I glued $16 worth of silk ivy, leaf by leaf. It looked like ivy was growing right out of the floor, and definitely softened that square opening.

Handmade Rug

Despite looking and looking, I couldn't find an area rug that was the right size and color. So I made a great big potholder loom, using two-by-twos and hundreds of nails, and wove a rug myself. This was a lot easier than it sounds. I went to a linen outlet and bought $60 worth of discount sheets in navy blue, yellow, rose and periwinkle. I cut the sheets into two-inch strips and wove them into a plaid pattern just like a big old potholder. I used a straightened coat hanger to pull the strips through.

Flea Market Finds

For my dining chairs, $12.50 each at an antique store, I made chair pads in the same yellow and cabbage rose pattern as the balloon shades. As an afterthought, I found a corner cabinet in the trash, painted it white, and set my teapots and pink china on the little open shelves. For under $150 I had the most adorable dining room.

Neighbors used to knock on my door bringing friends and relatives to see my house. They'd say things like "Look what she did with the ivy," "Where'd you get this rug?" and "I wish I could do this." I always waffled between telling how cheaply I decorated the house and just keeping my mouth shut.

CHAPTER 6

◆

THE FRUGAL WOMAN
Raises Her Family

We moved into a brand-new house three years ago, and I am still trying to organize my kitchen. But now that the boys are getting older, I don't want to spend all our time cleaning and organizing. I want to get out and enjoy life with them. I didn't become a mom so that I could perpetually pick up toys and clean the kitchen.

My plan for the winter is to pare down to the essentials. If something has some sentimental attachment or a *potential use in the future, it will be properly stored. Otherwise, it has to go. I dream of waking up to a clean and simple house, one that is a joy to be in, not a chaotic drain on my energy.*

I also want my boys to understand that the key to happiness is being comfortable in your surroundings, enjoying fully what you already have, and not just about acquiring more and new and better stuff. You can have fun just being and doing, instead of having and getting.

—*P.S.*

———◆———

BEING FRUGAL IS A FAMILY AFFAIR. AS THE FRUGAL Woman embraces a more pared-down life, her family, by extension, often does too. Children are taught by example, and as you set an example of responsible money- and stuff-management, they will learn from you. But raising children frugally offers benefits beyond just what your bank statement can convey. As you all focus less on material belongings, and more on creating rich experiences that rely on time spent together, you may discover your relationship with your family becoming deeper and more meaningful. And that is priceless.

The Frugal Woman Knows...

IT'S NEVER TOO SOON TO TEACH KIDS ABOUT MONEY

A Frugal Woman loves a good hand-me-down. What better to pass on to your children than wise lessons about finances?

Start them on the savings habit.

"When my daughter started getting a weekly allowance, from the beginning we insisted that 30 cents of each dollar go into her piggy bank. When she reaches a certain amount ($5), the money gets deposited in her bank savings account. I'm trying to teach her a three-tier system: one portion to long-term savings, one portion for short-term savings, and one portion for her to do with as she pleases."

———— ✦ ————

"I took my kids to the bank as soon as they could read, write, and do simple arithmetic, and opened bank accounts for them. When they would get money for birthdays or for doing chores, I had them put half the money in savings. They learned that money in the bank earns interest, and enjoyed seeing the small sums add up over time. By the time they were in high school they were able to buy CDs and savings bonds to save up for college. When they had some money saved up, they were allowed to withdraw no more than a fourth of it, once a year, for special things like doing their own Christmas shopping, buying clothes other than the ones I provided for them, or to spend on family vacations. That meant they had to plan how they would use their money."

———— ✦ ————

"I took my son to the bank, the real bank. He took his money to the teller, and handed it over himself. This was *his* experience. All 'big' purchases were his to figure out—he saved for six months to buy the video game system he wanted. Next step? His own mutual fund. It's never too early to start saving for retirement. Teaching them about money is like teaching them to go potty—you can put them on the pot, but you can't 'go' for them."

Teach them to be savvy consumers.

"From very early on I taught my kids that a bargain isn't a bargain if it's something you don't really want or need. My 17-year-old is a sale shopper now. He wanted name-brand shoes that were $125 at most stores. He finally found them in a catalog for almost half the price. We focus on things that we really want, and then get the best price we can."

———— ✦ ————

"I have started hearing 'everyone else has it' and 'everyone else is wearing it.' I explained to my oldest son that we are saving for a home of our own and that we have three children to put through college. He understands. If he wants expensive clothes or shoes, I tell him he can spend his own money. I get strange looks from him, but it has taught him the value of a dollar. Two days ago, we went to the Salvation Army to purchase clothes for our three boys. We bought a pair of sandals, a pair of name-brand shoes, two pairs of name-brand pants, a pair of jeans, eight pairs of shorts, two shirts, underwear, and a belt for $25. As we walked out the door holding three bags full of clothes, my oldest son's mouth was hanging open. He said, 'You got all of this for $25.' I proudly stated, 'Yes, for the price we would have paid for just one pair of pants in a department store.' Stick to your guns about the decisions you make to be frugal. And continue to teach your kids about money because you are educating them as much as their teachers do in school. When they are grown and living on their own, they will understand that you were right."

Start them on investments.

"I have 10 nieces and nephews, a wide range of ages. I buy 10 shares of stock in a company that the kids know about (like Coca-Cola, McDonald's, Kellogg's), and transfer one share to each of my nieces and nephews. With inexpensive online stock trades, this can be done very easily. This is one gift that always fits, and isn't broken by the end of Christmas day. It has educational value, not to mention financial value (usually) as the value of the stock grows."

The Frugal Woman Knows...

HER KIDS DON'T NEED *ALL* THOSE TOYS

Too much stuff is too much stuff, whether it's your own or the kids'. Certainly, no one would advocate taking a beloved doll or favorite baseball glove away from a child, but as you stare at the 15th Barbie or Rescue Ranger just added to your child's collection of rarely-played-with items, you might be thinking, *Do they really need all that stuff?*

Maybe not. Here's how some Frugal Women have approached the issue of simplifying and paring down their children's belongings.

Use literature to put things in perspective.

"I was reading *The Little House on the Prairie* books to my daughter, about how Laura got a penny, one piece of candy, a pair of mittens, and a doll for Christmas, and it was the biggest, best Christmas ever. It made me feel ashamed of how overindulged our kids are. Granted, many of the toys and things come from grandparents, but enough is enough! I'm tired of having so much stuff to clean, organize, and put away. Especially those darn toys (the kids' and mine!). I'm paring down because I know that we'll all be better off spending less money on toys and putting that money toward college funds, or even retirement."

Pare down by donating.

"I have two boys, and we get a lot of hand-me-down toys. Families have dropped off boxes full of toys for us. Needless to say we used to have entirely too much 'stuff.' I highly encourage giving away extra toys to a local shelter. Or feel free to pass them on to families with younger kids. One thing I started relatively early was a toy roundup. We go around the toy room with a basket and pick out toys that we are going to give to other babies or children that do not have fun toys to play with. We talk about giving, the benefits of it, and how the kids will probably feel playing with a new-to-them toy. I have talked with my kids about how much fun they got out of a toy, and how the time has come for us to pass along that goodwill. Find the reasoning that works for you and your kids."

"Recycle" toys.

"Here is something I would do when my kids were little. I would go through their room, bag up some toys, and put them in the attic. After six months, on a rainy day, I would bring the bag down. The kids loved it. It was like having new toys again!"

Teach them the value of time.

"We recently moved into a new house, and there is nothing more staggering than boxing up all your possessions. It forced me to look at everything we own and to say to myself, *Darn, we've got a lot of stuff*. I don't think that stuff is inherently bad. But even sentimental items create stress for me if they're left lying around. If my daughter wants to paint, I want to be able to quickly lay my hands on the supplies. I don't want to have to dig around for stuff. That stresses me out."

———— ◆ ————

"I really want my girls to understand that the greatest gift anyone can give is time. I want to teach them that a walk on the beach with Mom is so much more special than a trip through Toys "R" Us or the mall."

The Frugal Woman Knows...
TO TEACH HER CHILDREN ABOUT COMMERCIALISM

Television constantly barrages kids with ads for the latest "stuff." Here's how one Frugal Woman helped her children learn not to buy into the hype: "I watched television with my kids and explained what commercials were. I taught them that the advertisers will do or say *anything* to make you buy their product. This helped me to teach my kids that we don't buy everything on TV."

Another Frugal Woman was particularly concerned about the messages portrayed in commercials. She said, "I want my kids to know that they can be happy no matter what. I am sick of commercials that tell us if we want to be happy, we have to buy something. I particularly hate beer advertisements. When they come on, I talk with our teenage boys about the misguided message, that supposedly you will have beautiful women on your arm and be the life of the party if only you drink beer. Communication is essential to raising your kids right."

LESSONS LEARNED THE HARD WAY

Don't fool yourself into thinking that just setting a good example is enough to teach kids how to be financially responsible. To avoid the lure of easy credit, upfront discussion is necessary. Here's one (now) Frugal Woman's story of how a lack of parental direction contributed to her money mistakes.

When my husband and I were kids, we never learned about money. Whatever our parents wanted, they put on their charge cards. Money was never discussed, and budgeting was done in private. They talked about paying your bills on time and saving, but never showed us any real-life examples.

One month ago, we filed for bankruptcy. We had to cut up the credit cards, after accumulating over $40,000 in debt. Hospital bills (after a car accident) pushed our financial situation over the edge. My husband is still recovering. He had been working two jobs to pay our debts, but no more. My wages were being garnished. We had no choice other than bankruptcy–there was no way for us to even come close to our obligations.

My father was horrified when he found out that we'd had to declare. ('Oh, the shame that you've brought on the family!') He's still not speaking to me. He cannot understand how we got into this situation. *Didn't we learn anything from our parents' examples?* I told him that they never discussed money with us and never taught us to plan and manage a household budget. All that was done in private. Even today, I still don't know what my parents earn.

Do your kids a favor, and include them in the household budgeting before they leave home. Don't assume that they know what they are doing just because you think you set a good example. You may have set an example that you had not intended, or misled your children into thinking that life was easy.

My husband and I were under the impression that all newlyweds were in debt, and that all adults start out that way to pay for setting up your house. We thought that older people have more money, because they have paid their debt off. Our judgment was way off. Talk to your children about your finances. Help them get started on the right foot.

The Frugal Woman Knows...

HOW TO BEAT THE "I WANTS"

Even if your children are not the sort to regularly demand every item they see on TV (perhaps because you limit TV viewing in general), a trip to the store can often devolve into an outbreak of the "I wants"—"I want that candy!" "I want that toy!" "I want that shirt!" Here are five ways Frugal Women have found to head off spur-of-the-moment demands by their kids.

Be prepared.

"When I have to go shopping with my young kids, I make sure they are well fed and rested first. That assures me that they have plenty of reserves and will be able to follow directions, listen, and be reasonable. When they are hungry or tired, they tend to get distracted easily and act up in stores."

Set limits.

"When I go to the store with my kids, I explain to them in advance that we're not getting anything that's not on the list. If they are allowed to get something that day, I make it clear what that item is, or we set a dollar amount in advance."

Help them understand "No."

"When the 'I wants' start, for the most part I say no, and they realize when I mean it. If they ask why, I try to give them a tangible reason, such as 'We came to the store to buy your cousin a present, and it is not our turn today.' I think the secret to my success is that I have been consistent with my approach. No means no."

147

Have them pay for what they want.

"My daughter is six now, so the 'I wants' started last year. Now, when she says, 'I want such-and-such,' I ask her, 'Do you want this badly enough to spend your own money on it?' She has been saving for an item she saw at Target, and it is taking quite some time, so my question always makes her reconsider. Only once did she answer yes. Spending her own money has been educational for both of us. Now I know that if she wasn't willing to spend her own money on something, then she didn't want it that badly in the first place."

Avoid taking them shopping.

"It just got too overwhelming for us to take our two young kids shopping. We were bombarded with ads for toys wherever we went, even the gas station! Plus, out of guilt for 'dragging' them through stores, I would end up getting them a little something to be nice. So, to simplify things, we just stopped taking them into stores. We are even taking a break from the video rental store. This approach may seem radical, but it just wasn't worth the battles anymore. I was starting to feel angry because they had so much stuff, and I didn't want to cave in and get them anything else."

DEALING WITH TEENAGERS AND THE "GOTTA HAVE IT" SYNDROME

It may be easy to steer younger children away from commercial messages and the resulting demands for toys, but teenagers can be a different story. Here's how one Frugal Woman has kept her family—and budget—on an even keel as her son entered adolescence.

When my son was young, I would shop yard sales for toys and clothes. Now he is 12, and has 'woken up' from his innocence. He suddenly became aware of brands and what the other kids were wearing. Generic jeans were out! Name-brand sneakers were a must-have. Shopping became a nightmare. This is what I have figured out so far:

$ Keep buying from thrift stores, consignment shops, and yard sales. Just don't bring your kids along with you when you shop. Sneak the new items into the room—just place them on the bed or dresser. Hopefully, your child will focus on the 'gift,' and not where it came from.

$ Compromise. I will buy one expensive pair of jeans per season. That's it. All the rest must be reasonably priced. The child gets to pick what that item is. As much as I hate it, it is important for the child to feel he is on the same level as his peers and in style.

$ Postpone purchasing expensive items until birthdays and major holidays. Tell them that's when they can have those fancy sneakers or the video game.

$ Make them pay for it themselves. My son had to have a CD player, so I made him save for it. When he had saved the money, I took him to the store and he paid for it himself with the money he had saved from his allowance and assorted cat-sitting jobs. He was proud of himself. The worst thing you can do to your child (in terms of money at least) is to give them the impression that money appears effortlessly.

$ Do everything you can to limit your child's exposure to television. Be aware that they are being hit with advertising on the Internet too.

$ Refuse to buy them things you don't believe in—no exceptions. I refused to buy my son a Game Boy, so he bought one used from a friend and purchased the games himself with saved money. I will not allow the more elaborate systems into the house, even if he pays for them. Yes, they will come whining to you, but stand your ground if it's something about which you feel strongly.

The Frugal Woman Knows . . .

TO BE FRUGAL WITH HER FAMILY'S TIME

Soccer, ballet, chess club, music lessons, ice skating, hockey league . . . Are these just a few of the activities your kids are doing after school and on the weekends? Are your kids' schedules busier than yours? These are the questions that are troubling Frugal Women. It may be time to simplify things.

Balance organized and do-it-yourself activities.

"Some activities are good for kids. My husband and I would love to do sports with our kids, but some things we can't teach them ourselves, like gymnastics. The instruction helps them to develop their skills and abilities. But we also have a balance. We make plenty of time for doing things like swimming and other fun family activities. The kids get to practice their skills, but there isn't any instruction."

———— ✦ ————

"On the issue of electronic games, computers, and television, I don't think they're bad for kids, as long as they don't use them excessively. You are the parent, and you control the amount of time kids can spend with these devices. In this technological world, you may be doing your kids a disservice by keeping them away from it completely, particularly computers. My kids play on the computer and we have a couple of video games, but they also ride their bikes and do other outdoor games, and they even enjoy helping with family projects like gardening and washing the car."

Don't live vicariously through your children's activities.

"My daughter keeps telling me that she's bored and that all her friends are involved in 'activities.' I've tried to explain to her that when I was young and bored, I would make something to fill my time, like clothespin dolls, or write and illustrate my own little book. My friends and I didn't need in-line skates and scooters to keep busy. What ever happened to kids creating their own entertainment? Maybe it's the parents who are lacking in imagination. Think about it. If it weren't for such activities as soccer and ballet lessons, would we the parents feel important? Would we have a social life? Might we be forced to interact with our child? I'm not saying no to activities and organizations. But one or two per week, or a couple in the summer, seems ample. Maybe we parents should get our own social life. Try out an activity for yourself! As adults, we still need to cultivate ourselves through our own interests. Try out different things and see what suits you. Then you'll really have something to talk to the other soccer moms about."

Teach your children to entertain themselves.

"I always swore I would not be one of those moms whose life was just running kids from one activity to the next, and so far I'm (just about) holding my own. When my kids tell me they're bored, I tell them 'Good!' Some kids would love to be bored once in a while, but they're too busy running off to the next activity. I taught my kids how to entertain themselves. I actually overheard my son say that he just didn't understand why some kids like to sit in front of the computer all afternoon when they could be outside building forts and going on 'adventures' like he does. I am bringing my kids up to use their imaginations, and so far so good. When I was a kid (yes, the world was different then), my friends and I would take off on our bikes and not come home for hours. Kids today are getting burned out early, scheduled down to the very last minute of every day. Let them have the freedom to just 'do nothing' sometimes—that's what childhood is for!"

For a Rich Life . . .
FIND FUN FOR FREE

Wondering how to keep your children busy without shelling out for expensive lessons, electronic games, and trips to high-priced theme parks? Try one (or more) of these great activities.

Picnic in a local park.

"We live in a rural area and have a pond and a swing set. Even with that, my two young children (and I) get bored of the same thing all the time. What I do is drive them into town to one of the nice parks. They love it. I pack a lunch, or bring along a drink and snack. We alternate parks to make it 'different' each time. A change of scenery makes a world of difference to a little kid. And I love it because it's free."

Check into free admission days.

"We live in the city. Our neighborhood park and library were my salvation when my children were small. Now that they're a little older, once a week or so we take a subway or bus to a different park or library for a change of pace. We go to the zoo on its free admission day. Most zoos, museums, and so on have a free admission day once a week or once a month, so call around."

Hit the local library.

"Our library holds story hours for kids almost every day—it's great on rainy days or in the middle of winter when you want to get your preschoolers out of the house. Plus, the library has 'kids only' computers, where the kids can sign up for use by the half-hour, and use library copies of educational CD-ROMs like *Jump Start* and *Arthur.*"

Indulge in cool weather outdoor fun.

"Go leaf collecting—find some really cool leaves and preserve them in wax paper. Jump in a pile of leaves—how fun is that? Take a nice drive and look at the colored foliage. Roast marshmallows in the backyard together. Make a snowman, a snow fort, or snow angels."

Hold regular family nights.

"We rent movies and pop some popcorn instead of going out to the movies all the time. It's special for the whole family. We also play games (like cards or Monopoly) instead of watching television."

Plan a backyard campout.

"If you can't plan a camping vacation, just have a campout in your own backyard. If you already own a tent, it won't cost you anything. If not, see if you can borrow a tent from a friend."

PACK YOUR OWN SNACKS

Tired of spending too much on food at every family outing? One Frugal Woman shares her strategy:

When I'm out with the kids, buying drinks and snacks along the way can really add up. We also like taking day trips with the kids in the summer, and we tend to go places where you can bring your own food, like the beach. So I bought one of those big soft-sided coolers at a housewares store for about $6. I add a bunch of those reusable cooler packs, or a small freezer bag with ice inside a larger freezer bag works too. I pack juice boxes for the kids, and other drinks for the adults. I also bring along hard-boiled eggs, small chunks of cheese and crackers, veggie sticks, and maybe some sandwiches. Cold fried chicken is good too.

For a Rich Life...

MAKE YOUR OWN ARTS AND CRAFTS SUPPLIES

No need to spend big bucks in the toy store's craft aisle. You'll save money—and have more fun—by making your own. Here are some Frugal Women's do-it-your-self recipes for some favorite kids' art supplies.

Salt Dough

1 cup flour
1 cup water
½ cup salt
1 tablespoon vegetable oil
2 teaspoons cream of tartar

In a medium-sized pot, mix the flour, water, salt, oil, and cream of tartar together and cook over medium heat, stirring constantly until it forms a ball. Pour out, let cool slightly, and knead well.

Bathtub Paint

Can of shaving cream
Food coloring (variety of colors)

Squirt dollops of shaving cream into the sections of a muffin tin. Add a couple of drops of food coloring to each section, and mix with a spoon. Keep away from eyes.

Finger Paint

3 tablespoons sugar
½ cup cornstarch
2 cups cold water
Food coloring (variety of colors)
Liquid dish soap

In a saucepan over low heat, add the sugar and cornstarch and stir to combine. Add the water, and continue stirring until the mixture is thick. Remove from the heat. Spoon the mixture into sections of a muffin tin or individual cups. Add a drop or two of food coloring (a different color for each cup) and a drop of dish soap to each portion. Stir and let cool. May be stored, covered, in an airtight container.

Sidewalk Chalk

This chalk is not suitable for chalkboards, but it works great for sidewalk drawing, and it's more durable than commercial sidewalk chalk.

1 cup plaster of Paris
Disposable mixing bowls (like empty margarine tubs)
½ cup cool water
2 or 3 tablespoons tempera paint
Toilet paper rolls, one end covered with tape

Pour the plaster into a container. Add most of the water and stir. Add the paint and stir again, thoroughly. Add the rest of the water and stir again. Pour it into the toilet paper roll molds. Remove when thoroughly dry.

Goop

Toddlers love this oozy concoction.

> 1 box cornstarch
> Water
> Food coloring

In a dishpan-type container, add the box of cornstarch. Mix in some water, but not too much. Add food coloring (your choice). It should look like it would be solid, but when you pick it up it will ooze through your fingers.

Flubber/Blubber Stuff

This stretchy mixture is similar to Silly Putty. Kids go crazy over it (and more than a few adults think it's fun to play with too)!

> 1½ cups, plus 1⅓ cups, lukewarm water
> 2 cups white school glue
> Food coloring
> 3 teaspoons borax

In one bowl, mix together the 1½ cups water, glue, and food coloring (your choice of color). In a second bowl, mix together the 1⅓ cups water and borax. Pour the two mixtures together. Remove from the bowl, and knead until soft and consistent. Store in an airtight container.

Bubble Solution

1 gallon water
1 cup Joy or Dawn liquid dish soap
⅛ cup glycerin

In a large bowl or bucket, combine the water, dish soap, and glycerin, and stir gently.

A Frugal Woman Knows...
CARDBOARD BOXES PROMOTE IMAGINATIVE PLAY

Large packing boxes are the ultimate kids' amusement—easily turned into a playhouse, rocket ship, or whatever strikes their fancy, with some crayons and markers (and perhaps some help with scissors from you). Here are other ideas for boxes from Frugal Women.

Try a castle.

"I once made a castle-type house for a decoration years ago by starting with a couple of large Cheerios boxes for the base and building up, with cracker boxes glued to the outside edges for towers, and pudding boxes for brick walls. I used primer gray spray paint to cover it, and sponged a darker gray and white to faux-stone paint it. Toothpicks and felt were the banners. Your kids will love this."

How about a haunted house?

"My kids made themselves a haunted house out of bulk-sized cereal boxes. They cut them up and used packing tape to put it together. Then they drew some pictures on some paper and glued them on the house. It turned out really cute, and they're very proud of it."

Create a puppet theater.

"I took a large, sturdy shipping box, cut a door out of one side, and a window out of the facing panel. I let my daughter paint the outside, and we made a sign out of construction paper to hang in front, reading, 'Sammie's Puppet Theater.' She's had hours of fun putting on shows for her younger brother and me!"

FROM THE PANTRY TO THE PLAYHOUSE: HOUSEHOLD ITEMS THAT MAKE GREAT ART SUPPLIES

For inspiration, think back to the crafts of your own childhood—the things your mom kept you amused with before the days of 1,001 prepackaged craft kits. Or check out some kids' crafts books from your local library. Here are some mom-tested, kid-approved frugal craft ideas to get you started.

$ Paper towel and toilet paper tubes can be turned into play telescopes, rain sticks (seal one end, fill with rice or beans, seal the other end; when you shake it, it sounds like rain), and holiday figures.

$ Rice, pasta, and beans can be used to make mosaics.

$ Paper milk cartons (washed, of course) can be turned into dollhouses.

$ Wine and champagne corks can be decorated as little dolls.

$ Wooden clothespins can be turned into butterflies by securing a fanned rectangle of paper between the pinchers.

A Frugal Woman Knows...

HOW TO HOLD BIRTHDAY PARTIES AT HOME

Throwing a great party for your child needn't involve renting out an expensive setting, hiring overpriced entertainers, or shelling out big bucks for a bakery-made cake. These party ideas don't take a lot of money, just a little creativity. And they promise to be a lot of fun, because somewhere out there, a Frugal Woman has already thrown each one of these parties and worked out the kinks. So let the celebrations begin!

Call in the superheroes.

"I had a Batman party for my son when he turned three. I got really inexpensive black fabric and cording and made Batman capes for all the kids to wear at the party and then take home. They were a big hit. For a pin-the-tail game, we used a Batman poster and little pictures of cupcakes on poster board backed with mounting tape to play 'Feed the Cupcake to Batman.' For the cake, I made cupcakes and put a Batman ring that I had found at a party supply store in the middle of each one. Then I put them all close together on a platter. It looked really cool, almost like one big cake, but a lot less messy!"

Bring the circus to town.

"I had a circus theme for my three-year-old boy. I made felt vests by taking a long rectangle of felt and cutting a hole out of the center for the head. I also made collars out of white felt to make the neckline look a bit more clownish. I glued circles of felt in other colors down the front and glued a pompom on each spot. After the guests arrived we painted faces. Then they decorated plain party hats with colored dot stickers (the kind you can buy at an office supply store). The kids looked adorable and were very busy. I also made a picture of a clown on a piece of poster board with a big hole for a mouth. We tossed beanbags through the clown's mouth. They enjoyed doing this over and over."

Make your child king or queen for a day.

"We threw my son a 'royalty' party when he turned seven. The kids jousted with two pole-shaped gray pillows that I made. I cut the center out of two paper plates and put them around the end of the pillows to act as handles. Then they rode on broomstick horses with the shields they'd just decorated. (I cut the shields out of poster board, then we used duct tape to make handles.) We also 'slayed' a dragon-shaped piñata, and feasted on a castle-shaped cake—a sheet cake with cupcake towers, a graham cracker drawbridge, and a blue Jello moat."

Invite Arthur to the party.

"The children's television show *Arthur* is very popular with the kids around here. To have an Arthur-themed birthday, you could bake a big bow tie cake with some of the Arthur figurines on it. Then you could play 'Pin the Bow Tie (or Glasses) on Arthur.' Another good game would be 'D.W. the Picky Eater'—blindfold the kids and have them taste-test some foods and they have to guess what they are, such as spinach, catsup, lemons, and so on. Of course, you'd better check with the other children's parents to make sure there are no food allergies first."

Explore the great outdoors.

"A camping party, with the kids sleeping out in the backyard, is lots of fun. You can play flashlight tag once it gets dark. Or do a scavenger hunt in the backyard for items such as a stick, a small green leaf, a live ant, and a rock. Another fun game is the knot game: Have the kids form a circle and grab hands randomly across the circle. The object of the game is for the kids to untangle themselves, through teamwork, until they end up in a circle. For party favors, you could give out flashlights, a glow-in-the-dark light stick, or water bottles. You could even serve drinks in the water bottles and personalize them for each child with paint pens."

Play carnival games.

"When we had a little lull in the party activities, Dad stood holding a piece of poster board with a big hole cut in the middle. He put his face through the hole and the kids got to throw wet sponges at him. It was a big hit!"

For a Rich Life . . .
TEACH YOUR KIDS ABOUT GIVING BACK

You don't have to wait until Christmas to give back to your community. Better yet, you can involve your kids and teach them about volunteering while brightening someone's day at the same time. Here are some ideas from Frugal Women about involving their young children in community service.

"I started taking my two children to nursing homes. My young daughter (she was two when we started going) loved going to see her great-grandparents and visiting with the other residents. She of course was curious about wheelchairs, walkers, and other things, and she asked lots of innocent questions. Most residents loved talking with her and answering her questions. Children bring a lot of love and smiles to elderly people who are often extremely lonely."

———— ✦ ————

"Visiting a 'homebound person' or someone in a nursing home every week forms a strong bond of trust. In many cases we become their best friends. I've been visiting the same homebound person for three years now. She is an octogenarian widow with no children, and she lights up when I come through her door with my kids. The ongoing responsibility of visiting every week can be somewhat heavy—we can't move away, and I never know what condition I'll find her in, but being part of her life has been extremely rewarding."

———— ✦ ————

"We have the benefit of living right next to a nursing home. Both of my boys (ages one and five) love to visit. My older son will tell the residents about what he's doing in school or about his baby brother's new tricks. My one-year-old will walk into the cafeteria because he knows he can get lots of attention. Both boys are learning so much from our visits to the nursing home. About feeling good when you make others feel good. About giving of yourself, even if it's just a quick chat with each person. And about diversity and growing old—wheelchairs and oxygen tubes become less scary with each visit."

———— ✦ ————

"I've taken my girls to a local nursing home. The seniors loved the baby and had fun with my toddler. I think it is important to go visit the seniors and the sick throughout the year, not just at Christmas when they get most of their visitors."

RICH LIFE REWARDS:
A FRUGAL WOMAN'S TALE

Despite being raised in a family of eight closely spaced children, it was not until I married my husband, who grew up with parents who were raised very poor, that I got a sense of what frugal living really is. My mother-in-law learned that everything was valuable and to take care of everything you have, so you get the most use out of things.

My children are using their daddy's chair, wearing the bib overalls he wore as a child, and playing with his toy drum and wooden kitchen set—all are in great condition. When I realized that these things were not just saved for memories, but to be used by her children's children and, hopefully, their children one day, I realized frugal is very, very good.

Food in their home was also very valued because it was so scarce. I learned you can become a fabulous cook using leftovers. I also learned that homemade gifts and ornaments and things not bought in a store are priceless and must be treasured.

Because of growing up with parents like these, my husband knows the value of everything. He scans bargains at the store, and notices every mistake written on a price sticker. But it's not just about coupons and discounts. This family has taught me that living within these frugal means allows you to spend and save for things that you would think we would never be able to afford—like our honeymoon to a Caribbean island.

And one last thing this frugal family has taught me: To share this wealth of knowledge with others. When I see someone throwing something out, I stop them and let them know their options with it. Things kept, and kept well, are treasures.

—Mary Morgan, Sunbury, Pennsylvania

CHAPTER 7

♦

THE FRUGAL WOMAN
Celebrates Holidays

When I think of frugal living, I think of the many creative ideas that have been the result of this approach to living. I have been creative in my interests as years go by, but even though my income has grown, I have found that the creativity has remained because I have not been willing to simply spend whatever it takes to give gifts or have a beautiful home, inside and out. It is because of this that I believe that my friends and family can truly appreciate the *work and efforts I have put into the gifts I have shared and the different ways I have made my home truly special to my husband and myself. Gifts are always given with the person's specific interests in mind and so the creative financing—if you will—provides me the chance to find or create something truly unique that bears more value to the receiver than what I may have actually spent in actual funds. It takes effort to find or create just the right thing, but I am seldom at a loss for giving someone that little thoughtful gift that they really appreciate. That is just one of the priceless benefits of frugal living.*

—Carol Tiroff-Mazza, Margate, Florida

◆

CELEBRATIONS AND HOLIDAYS—ESPECIALLY THOSE FROM Halloween through New Year's—challenge everyone, frugal or not. Commercial culture would have us all believe that if we haven't given the largest bouquet on Mother's Day or bought "the" toy of the holiday season for every child on our gift list, that we've somehow failed as people. Frugal Women know that is not so.

However, the Frugal Woman loves to celebrate as much as the next person. She shows her decorating flair through what she makes herself, not what she can buy; she shows her wisdom through putting her energy into celebrating the event at hand, not draining herself by shopping madly.

HALLOWEEN

For a Rich Life...

MAKE YOUR OWN HALLOWEEN COSTUMES

Halloween has become one of the top-grossing holidays for many stores. Why? They've convinced many adults and children that the day won't be complete without an expensive pre-made costume. Take a step back, and remember the fun *you* had as a kid putting together something fabulous from scratch, and then help your kids feel the same by helping them to make their own costumes. And, after all, when's the last time a mass-produced outfit (which five other kids were also wearing) took a "Best Costume" award?

Here are 10 items around the house that you can use to make unique costumes.

1. If you've got sweat shirts and sweat pants...

"Get a white sweat suit. From there, your tot can be a dog, a cow, or a ghost. Just get some black felt, cut it in shapes and pin (or Velcro) the 'spots' to her suit! Add a little black eyeliner to the tip of her nose. For a dog, use the pencil to draw whiskers."

— ◆ —

"Attach balloons to a sweat suit and be a bunch of grapes!"

———— ✦ ————

"I bought a hooded black sweat shirt for my two-year-old girl and hand-sewed black felt triangles on the hood for ears and glued smaller white felt triangles inside the black ones. She wore it with black pants and shoes. I used eyeliner to draw whiskers. She was an adorable cat and wore the sweat shirt all winter."

———— ✦ ————

"Make a bird! I cut out poster board wings and tail and stapled on elastic bands. My daughter glued on hundreds of feathers, about $2 at Wal-Mart, and wore a blue sweat suit."

———— ✦ ————

"One son was a dinosaur. He wore yellow and green sweats with yellow socks over his shoes. We made the tail from one leg of an extra pair of sweats. We cut green and yellow sponges diagonally, then tacked the corners together and to the sweats to make the ridges of a stegosaurus running down his back and tail."

———— ✦ ————

"One of my kids' favorite costumes was a skeleton. They wore black sweat suits and white gloves. I cut bones out of white contact paper, peeled the back paper off and just stuck them on, painted their faces white and black, and off they went! When they were done, I peeled the 'bones' off the sweat suits and they wore the suits all winter!"

———— ✦ ————

"Last year my one-year-old son was a snowman. I bought a white sweat shirt and pants. We painted his face white, put black around his eyes, and gave him an orange nose. He wore mittens and a matching knit hat. For 'coal' buttons, I cut circles of sticky-backed black felt that could be removed easily from his sweat shirt after Halloween. This costume worked well because he stayed warm all night while trick-or-treating, and then we were able to use everything all winter."

2. If you've got hair gel . . .

"What's a quick and easy costume for the toddler? How about a 'baby greaser'? Use hair gel to slick his hair back, a white T-shirt, jeans rolled up, a comb in his back pocket and a jacket. We used a black raincoat from a thrift store but you can also use a jean jacket or similar."

3. If you've got cardboard boxes . . .

"Make a refrigerator out of a box. Cut out a hole at the top and two on the sides, and a door in the front. Glue pictures of food on the inside, so that when the door is opened, the fridge appears stocked."

———— ✦ ————

"When my sister and I were younger my parents made us into dice. They got a box for each of us, painted it white, cut out head and armholes, and then painted black dots on each side. I was six and on the front of my box were six dots, and my sister was two and so on the front of her box were two dots. I have also seen this done with dominoes (although that would be harder to sit down in, I imagine). We got tons of compliments and it cost next to nothing. Many stores will give away the boxes they have in storage!"

———— ✦ ————

"This is the easiest (and cheapest) costume I ever made for my daughter: I got a big box, took off the bottom, cut holes for arms and head, and wrapped it in gift wrap. Then, I taped ribbon around it, and tied lots of curly ribbons in her hair. Everyone raved about how cute and clever the costume was. I was thrilled that, after years of sewing, one with so little effort got such a result!"

4. If you've got bags . . .

"Get one of those orange, plastic, pumpkin leaf-bags and stuff it with newspaper. Place holes for your child's head and arms. Then staple the bottom together. Total cost: about 90 cents."

5. If you've got overalls . . .

"When my son was two, I dressed him in a pair of his overalls and folded up one of the pant legs about midcalf. I used a black makeup pencil and drew a few freckles on his face. He wore a baseball cap turned sideways. He was adorable."

———— ✦ ————

"This year my 10-year-old daughter will be a scarecrow. Blue overalls, a plaid shirt, bandanna, straw hat, raffia for the straw, a little face paint, and voila, one scarecrow."

6. If you've got pajamas . . .

"The Halloween that my son was two, I let him wear his Batman pajamas (which were actually given to him by an older friend, so I didn't even pay for them!). Jammies with feet in them lend themselves to all sorts of variations—add ears to make a bunny, paint his nose black and add whiskers for a lion, and so on."

7. If you've got poster board . . .

"Last year I had to make my seven-year-old a new costume at the last minute. My nephew was an M&M, so she decided to be an M&M bag. I put together two pieces of yellow poster board, a few paints from around the house, and some twine. I drew freehand the letters from an M&M bag, painted the poster board, used a paper punch to place holes at the top, and tied the two pieces of poster board together with the twine. It resembled advertisement boards people wore in the 1940s. She loved it and we received many compliments about how original it was. You have to cut the poster board down to fit your child. Total cost: $1.20!"

8. If you've got snowsuits . . .

"When my kids were little, I'd dress them in snowsuits (for warmth), stitch or pin felt ears to the hood, and add a simple tail to the back. Then I'd get out my makeup and paint on a cat face."

9. If you've got yarn . . .

"Add a little yarn on the hood of a sweat shirt or hooded coat. Paint on whiskers and a dark nose with eyeliner and you have an instant lion!"

10. If you've got panty hose . . .

"Panty hose stuffed with paper, socks, or other fabric makes for great 'tails'—perfect for all kinds of animal costumes."

SIX CHARACTER COSTUMES YOU CAN MAKE CHEAPLY

1. Cookie Monster

"Use an adult-sized blue shirt with the bottom middle sewn (or glued) to make leg holes. Then take a blue baseball cap and glue big white balls (Ping-Pong balls maybe) on it with big black circles for the eyes. Make a cookie bag to collect treats in. Glue or sew two pieces of light brown felt together, and use dark brown or black peel-off felt for the chocolate chips."

2. Franklin the Turtle

"Dress your child in green sweats. Tie a red bandanna around her neck. Have her wear a red baseball cap. For the shell, cut a circle out of poster board and cut a couple of holes in it to loop a ribbon through to tie it. Then, use spray foam insulation to cover the poster board. Next, paint over with green and brown spray paint."

3. A Lego Piece

"Get a big box, cut a hole in one end for the head, and two for the arms. The box should go down to about the knees. Spray-paint it any color. Paint six margarine tubs the same color as the box, and glue them on in two columns of three each, as you would see on a Lego."

4. The Cat in the Hat

"We found the hat at a carnival, but it can be purchased in any costume shop. Wear a black sweat suit as a base, and add white gloves and a white piece of felt attached to the neck area."

5. Tony the Tiger

"Get an orange shirt with hood about five sizes too big. Sew ears on the hood and make an orange tail; stuff and attach it in the logical place. Sew on a white muslin piece to the chest. Make tiger stripes over the whole thing with a black permanent marker. Wear a black turtleneck and black sweat pants."

6. An Oreo Cookie

"Take a cardboard box, cut it into two circles, spray-paint it black (but leave the letters O-R-E-O unpainted by covering the cardboard with cut-out letters on paper). Dress your child in white sweats. Tie the two circles together and hang them over your child's shoulders."

THANKSGIVING

The Frugal Woman Knows . . .

HOW TO SPREAD OUT THE WORK

Hosting Thanksgiving doesn't have to mean making a single huge outlay of cash at the grocery store the week before the big day. Nor does it have to mean a crazed day or two of pulling it all together yourself. Here are some ideas for managing your money and time, so you can enjoy the day.

$ Shop ahead of time and stock up as sales and coupons present themselves for holiday staples like flour, butter, sugar, and easily stored vegetables such as potatoes and onions.

$ Make and freeze some dishes (such as pies and piecrusts) ahead of time.

$ Don't shy away from asking your guests to bring something. Your guests will understand it's an enormous amount of work to do all the preparation, and more than likely would love to contribute a dish or two.

$ To make it easy on them and yourself, assign dishes—one Frugal Woman suggests using evite.com, an online invitation site (it's free!). "When you send 'evites' to people, there is a 'what to bring' option. When guests RSVP, they choose from a list of things the hostess has in mind for the potluck. That way there are no duplicates and people can pick and choose."

For a Rich Life…

CELEBRATE WITH GRACE

Thanksgiving is, after all, about giving thanks for whatever bounties we have in life. A meaningful way to bring the idea of giving thanks first and foremost to your table is to craft a special grace to be said at the start of the meal, either in addition to or instead of any typical one your family may use. If you (or the person who typically says grace in your family) is not a natural-born speaker or writer, try some of these ideas to help you along.

$ Include quotes from (or read in their entirety) favorite poems, biblical passages, or stories, especially ones having to do with giving thanks (of course) or gatherings of families and friends.

$ Ask each member of your table (ahead of time; it's not fair to put them on the spot) to think of the one thing they are most thankful for over the past year, and have each guest share their thanks one by one, around the table. Or have them write them on slips of paper and give them to the main grace-sayer, who reads them aloud.

$ Search the Web for examples (enter "Thanksgiving grace" into Google.com for the most up-to-date list of links out there) written by other families as well as professionals.

For a Rich Life . . .

Decorate with the Bounty of the Season

When celebrating nature's bounty, use simple decorations based on produce, flowers, or harvest themes for an inexpensive yet elegant look.

Create an edible centerpiece.

"Every Thanksgiving, for as long as I can remember, my mother has made a fruit centerpiece—and at the end of dinner, it got eaten! I now do this for Thanksgiving at my house. It's incredibly easy, and costs far less than splurging on a big centerpiece. Just fill your favorite bowl with apples, pears, and grapes—I build mine into a small pyramid. Begin with three or four apples on the bottom, place three or four pears on top (set them so that their stems point up, to get the pyramid effect) and then drape the grapes over them."

Go with gourds.

"For a centerpiece, get some of those little decorative gourds, available in most supermarkets. Pile them up in the middle of the table, perhaps around some candlesticks or a single pillar candle. If you are using place cards, you could also carefully slice the gourds about halfway through and use them to hold the place cards."

Create a pumpkin tea-light holder.

"Every Thanksgiving we take the small pumpkins/mini-pumpkins and carve out a spot in the top big enough for a tea light candle to slide into. Then we light the tea lights and use them on the tables. Very simple and makes dinner a little bit more special."

Make a garland of thanks.

"I began this tradition in my family in the Thanksgiving of 2001; after September 11th it was important to me to focus our thoughts on what gifts life had given us and get beyond the food. I cut out several leaves from autumn-colored construction paper, and have each member of my family write down the one or two things they are most thankful for. Then I string them into a garland and drape it over the doorway of our dining room, facing the table. I've kept the leaves from the past few years and add on the new ones. It helps us reflect on what the day is really about."

For a Rich Life . . .

MARK THE START OF THE WINTER HOLIDAYS WITH GIFTS FROM THE HEART

While Thanksgiving should be celebrated on its own merits, it's become a fact of life that the day does inaugurate the Christmas season. But this tradition, started by a Frugal Woman and her family, is a lovely way to make the transition into the winter holiday season about more than a trip to the mall.

I have a rather large extended family. We created our own special tradition. Each "woman of the family" makes little ornaments and we exchange them at Thanksgiving. (This year I'm making pinecone angels.) We sit around after Thanksgiving and talk about how we made them. We all end up going home with 12 or more handmade gifts to put on the tree.

The Frugal Woman Knows...

HOW TO STRETCH A THANKSGIVING DINNER

Frugal Women, as we saw in Chapter 3, are experts on turning leftovers into comfort food feasts. Eliminate possible guilt about spending a little extra for your Thanksgiving dinner by factoring in the meals you'll get out of the leftovers. Some ideas for what to do with the leftover bird, beyond the usual sandwiches:

Turkey Soup

Simmer the bird carcass in several quarts of water for one to two hours, along with some carrots, celery, and onions. After making the stock, add leftover meat, additional vegetables, and rice for a hearty supper.

Turkey à la King

This variation on chicken à la king is made by cooking cubed turkey with mushrooms and red peppers in a cream sauce.

Turkey Pot Pie

Cube leftover turkey and cook with carrots, peas, and pearl onions in a cream sauce. Add a biscuit topping and you have a wonderful meal.

Turkey Chili

Use your favorite chili recipe and simply substitute cubed turkey for the meat.

HANUKKAH

For a Rich Life . . .

CELEBRATE THE FESTIVAL OF LIGHTS IN SIMPLE WAYS THAT KIDS WILL LOVE

If the "eight days of lights" have turned into "eight days of gifts" with your family, try one of these ideas to refocus your kids on the spiritual, while still having fun.

Make an easy clay menorah.

"Use any type of clay that can be air-dried or baked dry. Give your child a big hunk of clay to work into a log or brick-like shape. While the clay is still soft, use a candle (of the same size you will use for Hanukkah) to make nine indentations in the clay. Let dry, and have your child paint it."

Share a menorah snack.

"Give a paper plate and nine marshmallows to each child. Have them spread peanut butter on the plate, then stick the marshmallows onto it. Let the children poke one pretzel stick (candle) into each marshmallow. Pretend to light the candles, say the prayer—then eat up!"

Do a Hanukkah grab bag.

"We have come up with a great tradition that seems to work well and cut down on an excess of presents and cost. Before Hanukkah each child decorates a paper grocery sack. When Hanukkah arrives, we wrap up eight small gifts for each child's grab bag. On every night of Hanukkah the children may take one gift from their grab bag after we light the candles."

Put on a Hanukkah pageant.

"Make the Hanukkah story come alive for your kids by having them act out the story. This is especially fun if cousins and grandparents will be celebrating with you. Costume the children in bathrobes or large shawls; make swords and shields for the 'Maccabees' out of cardboard and cover them in aluminum foil or gold-toned tissue paper. A grown-up can play King Antiochus so that none of the children feel odd about playing the 'bad guy.' If one child is much older than the others, he or she could act as the narrator while the younger ones act out the story."

Plan eight days of kindness and charity.

"As Hanukkah is the Festival of Lights, do what you can to be lights to the world. Sit down with your children and plan out eight days' worth of charitable activities. You could visit a home for the elderly, volunteer at a shelter or food pantry, or help out with a winter clothing drive. Simpler ideas could include writing letters and drawing pictures for older relatives and friends who live too far away to visit, or having older siblings read to younger ones at night."

CHRISTMAS

The Frugal Woman Knows...

DECKING THE HALLS NEEDN'T DECK YOUR BUDGET

The pressure to have the "best decorated" house during the holidays can unravel almost anyone. But before you spend a ton of cash on objects to get that "old-fashioned" look, consider *doing it* the old-fashioned way: Make your decorations yourself. As one Frugal Woman says, "What better resource than your children for inexpensive decorations? Paper chains made in red and green, ornaments made from Popsicle sticks, and inexpensive ceramic ornaments that you can hand-paint together. Holiday decorating can be a great bonding time for your family."

Decorate a large tin.

"Cover the outside of a large coffee tin or other large tin with wrapping paper, tie a ribbon around it, and fill it with spruce or pine boughs. Place the tin on the floor. Remember to water the branches regularly to keep fresh. You can even decorate the boughs with Christmas ornaments, lights, ribbon, or popcorn strings."

Make natural garlands.

"Make popcorn and cranberry garlands. You can string them yourself, or make it a fun family project."

String up holiday cards.

"Cut small pictures from old holiday greeting cards, punch holes around the edges, and loop ribbon or yarn to embellish and hang. You can also add glitter."

Make paper stockings.

"Cut the shapes out of construction paper, old fabric, or felt. Have your kids decorate them with glitter, pipe cleaners, markers, and anything lying around the house. Stuff them with old newspaper to make them fuller."

For a Rich Life . . .

TRY EASY, ELEGANT CHRISTMAS CRAFTS

The following projects result in decorations that will make your house look festive—and they make wonderful gifts as well.

Jingle Bell Wreath Ornament

Tie these wreaths onto packages, tree, large grapevine wreath, doorknobs, or hang them from the mantle. Use the wreaths as candle rings. Hang one in each of your windows. Make a dozen or so extra, and drop them off at the local nursing home.

Materials:
Pipe cleaners or heavy craft wire
Jingle bells (red and green work well together, available at most craft stores)
Ribbon
Small Christmas balls, bows, or other decorations
String or ribbon for hanging the ornament
Glue gun
Wire cutters or heavy-duty scissors

Directions:
First decide what size you would like your wreath to be. Cut the wire or pipe cleaner 2-inches longer than the desired size of the wreath. String the jingle bells onto the pipe cleaner or wire. Bend the jingle bell–covered wire into a circle. Twist the ends of the wire (or pipe cleaner) together to secure. Cut off excess wire.

Tie a bow at the top of the wreath, to hide the twisted wire. Tie on or hot-glue your choice of holiday embellishments, such as bows, balls, or mini-presents. Cut a 5-inch piece of ribbon or string. Slip the string through the wreath and tie the ends together, and hang the wreath from the loop.

Snowman Can

Turn your empty coffee can into a snowman-themed decoration or a candy or gift holder. When done with this project, fill the snowman up with homemade cookies or candy, snap on the lid, and give it as a gift.

Materials:

Clean, dry coffee can and lid

Craft paints

Felt buttons

Craft foam (sold in sheets at craft stores)

Wire, ribbon, or string

Newspaper

Ice pick or awl

Hammer

Hot-glue gun

Directions:

Cover the work area with newspaper. Using the ice pick and hammer, punch a hole in the side of the can, about a quarter inch from the open top of the can. Make another hole exactly opposite from the first. Use the hammer to bang down any sharp edges.

Paint the entire outside of the can white, and allow to dry. Use the hot-glue gun to coat the edges of holes you made with the hammer and pick, taking care not to block the holes in the process.

Cut the foam into the shape of a hat, scarf, eyes, and nose. Glue the scarf about a third of the way down from the top of the can. Glue the eyes, nose, and hat above the scarf area. Glue on three buttons, vertically down the middle of the snowman. Cut little circles of felt or foam and use them to form the snowman's coal mouth. Allow to dry.

Thread the wire, ribbon, or string through the holes and tie to secure. This is your handle.

Snowman Sculptures

These snowmen look cute on the mantle. Children love doing anything that involves clay or dough.

Materials:
2 cups Ivory Snow detergent
½ cup water
Craft glue or hot-glue gun

Decorations:
Toothpicks, Popsicle sticks or small sticks, buttons, felt scraps, small beads, yarn, pipe cleaners

Directions:
Make your "snow" by mixing the Ivory Snow with the water and beating it with a hand-held electric mixer until it is the consistency of dough. Immediately shape into three balls: a large one for the base, a mid-size one for the body, and a small one for the head. Use toothpicks to hold the balls together as you stack them on top of each other.

Attach the decorations with glue. Use twigs or Popsicle sticks for arms and buttons or small beads for eyes. Make a scarf out of felt scraps or crochet a yarn chain. Use pompoms and pipe cleaners to make earmuffs. An orange pipe cleaner cut and folded into a small triangle forms the nose.

For a Rich Life...

SPICE UP YOUR HOLIDAY

Rather than shelling out big bucks for scented candles and prepackaged potpourri, raid your kitchen cupboard for easy, all-natural ways to put the scent of Christmas in the air.

$ Cut a 6-inch square out of cotton Christmas print fabric. Place a vanilla bean, 2 whole nutmegs, 10 whole cloves, and 4 cinnamon sticks in the center of the fabric. Gather up the fabric to enclose the spices and tie with one end of a 2-foot-long gold ribbon. Tie the other end of the ribbon to a doorknob. Whenever the door is opened or closed, the scent will be released into the room.

$ Stud oranges or pomegranates with whole cloves; display in glass bowls.

$ Fill a small bowl with spices: whole cloves, whole nutmeg, vanilla bean, cinnamon sticks, and strips of orange peel. Tie a ribbon around the bowl or place a bow inside the bowl and place it on a shelf or coffee table.

$ Simmer spices in a pot of water on the stove. Use whole nutmeg, cinnamon sticks, whole cloves, and vanilla bean.

12 Days of . . . Easy Ornaments

You can be sure a Frugal Woman's true love would not be giving her dozens of birds and singing, dancing, drumming, piping people to have to take care of after Christmas was over. But simple, inexpensive ornament ideas? You know that wins our hearts! Note: Some of these crafts require the use of a hot-glue gun. Be sure to supervise children during these activities.

1. Glitzy Icicles

Wrap a sparkly pipe cleaner around a pencil. Pull out the pencil and bend one end of the pipe cleaner into a hook.

2. Framed Picture

Glue a small photograph of your child or children onto a piece of cardboard. Glue new crayons around the edges for a frame. Add a ribbon hanger.

3. Reindeer Face

Bend a brown pipe cleaner into a V shape. Hot-glue the pipe cleaner to the base of a large colored Christmas lightbulb so that the tip of the bulb points down from the V. Curl the ends of the pipe cleaner around a pencil to create antlers. Glue a tiny bell onto the base of the V. Glue eyes and a red pompom nose onto the lightbulb. Add the ribbon at the very end of the base of the bulb to hang.

4. "Jeweled" Balls

Hot-glue clear or colored flat-backed gems onto glass Christmas tree balls. Create a pattern or glue them on randomly.

5. Glitter Balls

Mist glass ornaments with a spray adhesive and roll in glitter. This is also a great way to give new life to colored balls whose paint may have begun to chip.

6. Sequined Balls

Using pushpins with beaded heads, attach sequins to a Styrofoam ball. Add a loop of ribbon at the top, for hanging.

7. Fans

Fold a 2 x 2-inch piece of foil wrapping paper into a fan shape. Punch a hole in one end and tie with ribbon to hang on the tree.

8. Spice Balls

Fill clear glass ornaments with cinnamon, apple, or pine potpourri, and hang with a ribbon bow.

9. Jingle Cones

Spray-paint mini-pinecones in gold. Tie tiny jingle bells onto red curling ribbon; glue ribbon with attached bells to base of the cone, and hang by the ribbon when dry.

10. Star Brights

Cut star shapes out of cardboard and felt. Glue felt onto cardboard piece. Glue sequins to the edges.

11. Candy Canes

Twist red and white pipe cleaners together, barber pole style. Hook one end like a candy cane and hang on a tree limb.

12. Button Wreaths

Cut a plastic lid into a doughnut shape (round with a hole in the middle). Glue on green and white buttons and hang with a red bow. Paint wooden stars with gold glitter or wooden bells with silver glitter and attach to the wreath with glue.

For a Rich Life . . .

CELEBRATE WITH TRADITIONS THAT DON'T COST A THING

Give your family an old-fashioned Christmas that emphasizes the joy of spending time together at home, rather than at the mall. Here are some ideas for creating a cheer-filled holiday that won't leave your bank account with a hangover.

$ Choose one night to drive through a local neighborhood or park with spectacular light displays. Come home to hot chocolate and cookies.

$ Go caroling at a local nursing home.

$ Gather your family around or invite friends over to watch a holiday classic such as *It's a Wonderful Life, Miracle on 34th Street, The Grinch Who Stole Christmas,* or *A Charlie Brown Christmas.*

$ Read a favorite Christmas story aloud to your family (be they young or old).

RICH LIFE REWARDS:
A FRUGAL WOMAN'S TALE

When my husband and I first got married, we had nothing—just a chair and a bed. But we were happy. Our first Christmas we had a choice of a few small presents or a Christmas tree. We opted for the tree. My children didn't get toys and things during the year, only on birthdays and Christmas. Times have changed. My husband has his own business now and we have more than enough money. That is what I love about being frugal—that I can say *more than enough money*.

I love the fact that my kids don't constantly ask for labels and brands and everything they see at a store. I love getting an outfit at a thrift store or Wal-Mart and having people tell me I look great. I love teaching my children to use cash, not credit. If you don't have the money, you don't need it. That is my favorite thing about being frugal—teaching my children that it's what you need that is important, not what you want! And that what you need to get through life happily can't be bought in a store.

—Carol Keller, Mesquite, Texas

CHAPTER 8

◆

THE FRUGAL WOMAN
Gives Gifts

I enjoy making homemade gifts. To me, giving and receiving something made from the heart is priceless, and so thoughtful. It has a value that money cannot replace. I enjoy putting time into my projects, and I get so much back in return when I see how it lights up their faces. For that hard-to-buy-for person, I can wrap up some homemade muffins and loaves with some homemade apple cider mix, a couple of mugs, a cinnamon stick, a little votive holder *with a candle, all put nicely into a little basket, wrapped in cello wrap with a ribbon and bow, and directions on how to make the hot apple cider with a little apple juice in the microwave. It's just something nice and warm to enjoy while you curl up with a book, or relax in a hot tub—something to pamper yourself with. We all need to slow down and relax in such a fast-paced, stressful world, and to me what is better than relaxing doing crafts for a little "me" time.*

—Shelley Power, Truro, Nova Scotia, Canada

◆

WHETHER IT'S YOUR BEST FRIEND'S BIRTHDAY OR YOUR sister's first Mother's Day, chances are that any given month has at least one occasion that demands a gift for someone. While it often seems that gift-giving has become an excuse for commercial (and spending) excess, the Frugal Woman conveys her fondness for the intended recipient through gifts extravagant in their thoughtfulness, not their price. So rather than dreading the next "must-give" event, look for ways to really prove the old adage "it's the thought that counts." For is there really anything richer than a look of delight on another's face when he or she opens a gift that shows that someone really cares?

The Frugal Woman Knows...

HOW TO BE CREATIVE AND CRAFTY WITH GIFTS

One way to beat spending excessively on gifts is not to leave gift getting to the last minute. Making lovely handcrafted items as you have time, and keeping them in a dedicated drawer or box allows you to pull out a hostess gift right before going out, for instance. But we're all caught short at some time, so it's worthwhile to have a few quick-and-easy tricks up your sleeve. Here are eight super-simple gift ideas—ones that you can do ahead, as well as make at (almost) the last minute—for any occasion.

Homemade Tablecloths

"If you can sew, homemade tablecloths make a great gift idea for almost any holiday."

Sachet Bags

"Buy a bag of potpourri and some tight lace. Cut the lace into squares, fill with potpourri, and tie closed with ribbon to make little sachets."

Hand-decorated Frames

"When you aren't sure what to get someone, or need a last minute gift, take a plain wooden picture frame and paint it yourself. You can write someone's name, make little pictures, or even glue things on it."

Quote Books

"A quote book is a personal—and economical—idea! I bought a pretty journal and then scoured the Internet for inspirational quotes. The recipient will appreciate the time, effort, and thoughtfulness. Leave the second half of the book blank so he/she can add their own quotes."

Birdhouses

"Unfinished birdhouses are very affordable. I thought it would be a fun idea to buy a few and paint them myself to match the house of a friend or family member."

Painted Crates

"I found wooden CD crates at the dollar store for just 99 cents each. They can be stained, painted, or decorated any way you like, such as stenciling or decoupage. I fill them with affordable items according to certain themes. For example, in one I put a mug, tea bags, and cookies. I filled another with office supplies like pencils, pens, and note pads. Bath items work great too."

Home-decorated Candles

"I recently found out how easy it is to make customized candles. Start with a box of votives from the dollar store. Shred the votives using a kitchen grater and place them in an empty coffee can. Set the can in a saucepan filled about a third of the way with water. Heat the water gently; do not allow it to come to a boil (the wax could catch on fire). You can add scents, color, herbs, spices, flowers, seashells, or just about anything you want to the melted wax. (You can even add a crayon to the wax to color it.) Then take a thick glass (from the dollar store), in whatever shape you desire, and pour the melted wax into the glass, with a thick wick in place. When the wax has cooled, put the candle in the refrigerator for 24 hours. The candle then pops right out of the glass. You can decorate the outside of the candle now. For example, dip some holly leaves in melted wax and stick them to the outside of the candle. Wrap the finished candle in cellophane with a large ribbon or bow."

Personalized Stationery

"Use your computer to create personalized stationery (sheets and envelopes). I used clip art that was meaningful to each recipient, like a gardening woman for a friend who has a big garden. You can also create customized note cards, funky personalized address labels, business cards, and more."

For a Rich Life . . .
Make Your Own Gift Baskets

Those prepackaged gift baskets always look lovely in stores, and for those with more money than time, perhaps offer a frugal time savings. But you can create your own—and make them truly match the recipient—with little effort. Here's how one woman does it: "For a romance basket, I burn my own CD—a compilation of great sexy and romantic songs. Along with the music, I add a fragrant votive candle (from an assortment pack), a mini-bottle of wine (they come four to a pack, enough for four baskets!), or a pack of hot cocoa, depending on the person, and a nice glass or mug. You can find nice and unusual mugs and glasses on the clearance shelf of most stores."

Another Frugal Woman recommends shopping around: "Try discount stores like Marshall's: They have all kinds of 'treasures' lying around—unmatched teacups, votives, statues, glasses—you name it. I like to pick through the stuff and find a few items that have a common theme. Then I'm off to the craft store to buy a cheap box. I paint the box to match the theme of the treasures I found. For fun you can throw in some candles, body wash, spices, candies, cookies, specialty teas, or whatever."

The Frugal Woman Knows . . .

WHAT TO GIVE THE SPECIAL PEOPLE IN HER LIFE

Look to your friends' and family members' passions for inspirations for meaningful, yet budget-wise, gifts. Try these ideas for easy and fun presents.

For the Movie Lover

"Get a big bowl from the dollar store and fill it with popcorn foam (to make it look like popcorn), then add several packs of microwave popcorn, boxed candies (the kind you buy at the movies such as Raisinettes or Goobers), and a gift certificate from your local movie rental place. Wrap the bowl in colored plastic wrap and tie with a ribbon."

For the Cook

"Everyone loves those flavored cooking oils you see at gourmet stores, but no one likes the prices, so I started making my own. Buy a gallon-size container of vegetable oil at the supermarket and a smaller bottle of olive oil from the dollar store. Use some pretty iced-tea bottles (for instance, from SoBe or Arizona) for bottling your oils. Just clean them really well and soak off the labels. Add various spices to each bottle. My favorite is a combination of dried red chiles, rosemary, and oregano. Then fill each bottle three-quarters of the way with the vegetable oil and the rest with olive oil. Let them sit for three to four weeks for mild flavor or up to three to four months for a really rich deep flavor. We spend less than $20 and can make 6 to 10 bottles of oil. Try adding sesame seeds, tarragon, and a pinch of soy sauce for a really good Asian-style dressing."

———— ◆ ————

"My husband makes a mean barbecue rub. You can buy spices in bulk, and you can probably pick up some cheap spice shakers at the dollar store. We make up a big batch of the barbecue rub, fill the spice shakers, and wrap ribbons around them. Make some cute labels on the computer. If you don't have a secret barbecue rub recipe, just mix up some cinnamon and sugar."

———— ✦ ————

"Know someone who likes to cook but doesn't have a lot of time for food shopping? Buy an unfinished wooden or ceramic bowl and paint it yourself. Then fill it with all of the items needed to prepare a favorite dish like pasta or gumbo."

For the Beauty Queen

"Find some small bottles with caps or stoppers. Buy large bottles of nice-smelling bubble bath and bath salts and fill the small bottles. Tie ribbons on them, and add a small ornament if you can."

———— ✦ ————

"Buy large gift packs of bath products at the wholesale/price club and divide the contents between two or more people on your gift list. You can keep the container for yourself and wrap the gifts in cellophane bags and tie with ribbons."

———— ✦ ————

WAKE UP AND SMELL THE (FLAVORED) COFFEE

These flavored coffee mixes make a great present for coffee lovers. Pack them in zipper-top plastic baggies, or small canning jars decorated with ribbon.

Café Bavarian Mint Flavored Coffee

¼ cup powdered creamer

⅓ cup sugar

¼ cup instant coffee

2 tablespoons baking cocoa

2 hard candy peppermints

In a blender, combine creamer, sugar, coffee, cocoa, and peppermints. Process until well blended. Store in an airtight container. Include a label or note that says: "Café Bavarian Mint Flavored Coffee: Stir in 2 to 3 tablespoons per cup of hot water."

Café Viennese Flavored Coffee

¼ cup powdered creamer

⅓ cup sugar

¼ cup instant coffee

½ teaspoon cinnamon

In a blender, combine creamer, sugar, coffee, and cinnamon. Process until well blended. Store in an airtight container. Include a note or label that says: "Café Viennese Flavored Coffee: Stir in 2 to 3 tablespoons per cup of hot water."

"Making homemade soaps turns out to be a lot more economical than buying fancy soaps, not to mention the personal satisfaction of giving gifts that I made myself. I bought a soapmaking kit for about $22, which includes one white soap base and one clear soap base, a set of eight different-shaped molds, two different fragrances, and two bags of color chips (used to dye the soap). Technically, that's everything you need to make several bars of soap. However, I like to add things, such as oatmeal flakes, almond slices, seashells, etc., to make soaps that have little 'surprises' inside. The rough textures are great for the skin—they help exfoliate dead skin cells."

———— ✦ ————

"Oatmeal bath pouches make a wonderfully soothing bath. I've used sandalwood scent, ylang-ylang, and patchouli. Peppermint or eucalyptus will soothe a chest cold, as will rosemary. A blend of orange blossom and lemon helped little cousins with their chickenpox itches. A variety of bags made out of fabric scraps, arranged in a basket would be cute. To create this gift, make small cotton/muslin drawstring bags roughly the size of a bar of soap (or buy muslin tea bags). Measure out enough dry oatmeal to fill the number of bags you have. I use about ½ to ¾ cup per bag. In a nonporous bowl, mix the oatmeal with a few drops of essential oil of your choice. You do *not* want a moist or damp mixture. Stir the oatmeal (or cover and shake) so the scent is mixed throughout. Fill the bags and knot tightly. Oatmeal in the bath drain is a bad thing, so be sure your bags are closed. To use, simply toss one bag into the bath as the tub is filling. Squeeze a few times to wring out scented oatmeal juice."

Bath Salts

Materials:

12 tall jelly (12-ounce) canning jars with lid and rings, washed and dried

Two 4-pound cartons Epsom salt (approximately 16 cups)

4 pounds sea salt or kosher salt (approximately 6 cups)

½ teaspoon glycerin, divided

2 pieces card stock (for tags)

For Candy Cane Bath Salts:

12 to 15 drops peppermint essential oil

12 to 15 drops red food coloring

For Peaches and Cream Bath Salts:

12 to 15 drops peach essential oil

12 to 15 drops orange food coloring

Directions:

In large mixing bowl, empty one carton Epsom salt. Add 3 cups salt and stir well. Stir in ¼ teaspoon glycerin and 6 to 8 drops essential oil. Mix well.

In the mixing bowl of a heavy duty stand mixer, empty one carton Epsom Salt. Add 3 cups salt and stir well. Add ¼ teaspoon glycerin, 6 to 8 drops essential oil, and food coloring. Set mixer to lowest setting and mix until color is even.

Holding canning jars at an angle, layer salts in jars, alternating white and colored mixtures. Seal the jars.

Cut gift tags apart and attach to jars. On gift tags, write the name of the bath salt and "Use 2 to 3 table-spoons for a refreshing bath."

Makes 12 12-ounce gift jars (plus 3 to 4 cups extra bath salts, which you can package in small plastic zipper-top bags for easy stocking stuffers).

For Children

"For my four- and seven-year-old nieces, I thought it would be a great idea to get plain canvas bags (the ones people use to carry groceries) and decorate them myself. I have sewn little starburst bead patterns on them and plan on getting some fabric paint to paint some neat designs. The bags were only $2 each and the amount of money I spend on decorating is solely up to me. I'm calling them library bags so the girls can keep all of the books they check out in one safe place. My sister thought it was a great idea since she's always paying late fees at the library."

———— ✦ ————

"My gift to my four-year-old nephew will be his first trip to the art museum. After our visit, I plan to find images of the artwork on the Internet and print out copies so he can start his own 'art collection.'"

———— ✦ ————

"I bought a red child-size canvas apron and some fabric paints. I decorated the apron with the girl's name, a flower, and a few paint dots. Total cost: under $9. Taking the time to personalize a gift for anyone makes it more special."

———— ✦ ————

"Choose a nicely decorated glass or mug and fill it to the brim with different kinds of chocolates, lollipops, and other treats, and wrap them in colored cellophane."

———— ✦ ————

"Kids love tie-dye shirts, especially when you make them matching socks!"

For Teens and College Students

"Teenage girls are the hardest people to shop for. This year I bought a cheap box at the hobby store and filled it with things like silly pencils, candy, key chains, smelly stuff like lip balm, hair bands, and note pads. I bought everything at the dollar store."

———— ✦ ————

"My daughter is in college. One of her favorite gifts from me was a goody box I put together, filled with things like stamps, gasoline/fast-food coupons, snacks and cookies, hot chocolate, shampoo, toothpaste, a roll of quarters for the Laundromat, socks, and hand lotion. She needs these things throughout the year and she appreciated having them on hand when her school schedule got to be hectic."

———— ✦ ————

"Get a $10 gift card from Blockbuster, a bottle of their favorite soda, a package of microwave popcorn, and of course some candy."

———— ✦ ————

"When your kids go away to college, you can make them a scrapbook. Start with one of those binder photo albums with the plastic sheet protectors. Fill it with memories of your child growing up. You probably have a few boxes stashed away with report cards, school play programs, concert tickets, photographs, awards, and so on, that would be perfect for the scrapbook. Add notes on cards with your own personal memories."

———— ✦ ————

"Buy a variety pack of nail polish. Divide them up and make small gift baskets with two bottles per girl, or whatever works best. Add some cotton balls, nail polish remover, emery boards, and nail clippers. You can even buy those pretty bottles with stoppers and divide a large bottle of polish remover between several bottles."

———— ✦ ————

"Jean purses make a great gift idea for teen girls. Cut the back pockets off an old pair of jeans. (Remember—never let anything go to waste!) With the fabric facing inside out, sew two pockets together along the bottoms and sides, leaving the top open. When finished, turn the purse right side out. Take some ribbon or other fabric and make a strap. Decorate it, and add a zipper or a snap to keep it closed."

Easy Holiday Gift Bags for Kids and Teens

If you have many young people on your Christmas list, finding and purchasing gifts for all of them can be overwhelming. Here's one Frugal Woman's ingenious solution.

I put together Christmas bags for each child. They are easy to fill up since the items inside don't have to be expensive, just fun. Here are some ideas for different age groups:

For Young Kids
Candy, memo pads, neat pencils/pens, erasers and sharpeners, stickers, toothbrushes, and, if the child is not too young, beads and some string to make friendship bracelets.

For Teen Girls
A small lotion bottle, small refresher spray or perfume, barrettes, body glitter, lip balm or lip gloss, a small hairbrush and/or mirror, temporary tattoos, and makeup brushes.

For Teen Boys
A sample-size cologne/aftershave, a small can of shaving cream and razor, and a coupon for a video store.

For Grandparents

"I found a bunch of photographs of my kids, and I'm making a collage for each set of grandparents. If they're old enough, kids can help with this project."

——— ✦ ———

"Make footprints or handprints out of plaster of Paris. Pour the plaster into a paper plate, and then make the prints. Let them dry overnight and have the kids paint them with finger paint or watercolors. It's an inexpensive gift, but grandparents will treasure it for a lifetime."

——— ✦ ———

"All four of the grandparents in our family are still living, and buying gifts for them is really hard. Here is a great frugal basket idea. In each basket include a coffee cup, a few chocolate-dipped spoons, some coffee singles (they look like tea bags), and some homemade cookies."

——— ✦ ———

"I have a 15-month-old son, and his grandparents are all over the country, so they don't get to see him much. I had him paint and scribble pictures on white construction paper. Then I cut out the pictures and put them in one of those picture frames with a bunch of separate photo spaces. I put a picture of him in one of the frames. We made one of these for each set of grandparents, and they loved it."

For Guys

"These are some ideas that my husband has loved: blank CDs (for his CD writer); a lighted screwdriver, available at the auto parts store—very neat and it makes working on things like computers much easier; a gift card for an electronics store where he already shops like Best Buy or CompUSA."

——— ✦ ———

"I make baskets every year for guys, and you wouldn't think that men would appreciate this type of thing but they do. Include bath items like bars of soap, shampoo, shaving cream, razors, and trial-size colognes."

——— ✦ ———

"You can always get him a mouse pad personalized with a photograph. Almost any film-developing store can do this relatively cheaply. I'm giving my father one with a photo of his grandchildren."

——— ✦ ———

"Make him a coupon book (you can print it from your computer) for time alone with you including a romantic dinner, massages . . . you get the idea."

——— ✦ ———

"I work at a Web hosting facility with a lot of techie guys. Most of them like comics, cool music, action figures, and especially DVDs. The best gift for them is a gift certificate to a DVD or software store."

For Family

"A nice idea for inexpensive gifts for family is to make copies of special family photos. I found an old photo of my mother and her family at an aunt's wedding.

I took it to the local photo shop and got color copies made. I put them into affordable frames and had special gifts for my brother and sister."

———— ✦ ————

"I always get the free double prints when I develop film, leaving me with a ton of extra pictures of the kids. I figured out a way to use them to make adorable magnets to give to family and friends. I cut off most of the background excess around the kids, glue it to watercolor cold-press paper, place a piece of laminating paper over the top of the picture and cut out the kids closer (for example, in between the legs, right up against the hairline). Glue a heavy-duty magnet on the back and voila! It's a thoughtful gift that also has a useful purpose. I spent just $20 on a pack of 50 magnets, the watercolor and laminating paper, and glue."

———— ✦ ————

"My husband and I just bought our first house, so our budget for Christmas was really low. For my mother and father, I wrote poems capturing childhood memories. I wrote them in pretty blank cards. I know they will appreciate them more than any expensive gift I could give."

For Teachers

"Homemade bread and cookies in a little tin are nice."

———— ✦ ————

"As a teacher, I can tell you that every year we are inundated with apples, apple mugs, apple books, apple frames, and apple crafts. Here is a list of the best gifts I've gotten:

$ Movie rental gift cards

$ Candles, potpourri, and anything that smells good and is relaxing

$ Bookstore gift certificates

$ Gift certificates to the local coffeehouse or bagel shop

$ Volunteers have brought us lunch from 'the outside'—cafeteria food doesn't make for a very exciting meal.

Another approach that's easy on the parents—and that we teachers love—is for the parents to each donate a few dollars and, with the pooled funds, purchase a gift certificate to a home-decorating store, restaurant, or department store."

———— ✦ ————

"If your budget is really low, write the teacher a letter telling him or her how much you appreciate the good job being done, what the teacher means to your child, that kind of thing."

———— ✦ ————

"Make little 'Teacher Therapy' gift baskets, with herbal tea, chocolate, bubble bath, and a scented candle."

For Coworkers

"Make a hard-candy wreath to hang at the office for everyone to enjoy. You can make the wreath form out of a wire coat hanger. Just bend the hanger into a circle. Buy a few different bags of wrapped candies that are twisted at each end, like mints, Tootsie Rolls, butterscotch disks, and sour balls (great for color). Tie a piece of curling ribbon around the end of one of the twisted ends of the candy, leaving enough for curling at the end. Once the candies are all ready to go, start tying them around the wire wreath that you made with the hanger. You can easily do this at night relaxing in front of the TV. As you go around the wreath with the candies, and slide them down as you go, they will all bunch together eventually to form a nice fat wreath. I like to curl the ribbon after all of the candy is on the wreath. Hang the wreath and tie a pair of scissors to it (out of the reach of children of course) so that people can cut a piece of candy off whenever they'd like."

———— ◆ ————

"Make an office survival kit. Find a cheap box or basket and toss in a travel size of Static Guard, scented hand lotion, funny Post-it notes, nail files, breath mints, candy bars, and tea bags or cocoa packets."

For a Rich Life . . .

GIVE THE GIFT OF CHARITY

Many Frugal Women have found that the most meaningful gift they can give is not something material but a donation to their friends' favorite charities. Not only does it allow you to do good, but it also tells your friends you support their values. Here's how one Frugal Woman does it: "I have a lot of friends. I choose a charity that each friend believes in, and make a donation in his or her name, usually for just $5. The charity sends a note that a donation has been made in their honor but doesn't state how much it's for. It's a way to remember a good friend while contributing to a good cause."

For a Rich Life . . .

SHOP YEAR-ROUND FOR HOLIDAY GIFTS

Frugal Women have found that shopping for holiday gifts year-round not only saves money, but their sanity, as well. As one crows, "Whenever I see a sale I buy then, especially for relatives, teachers, and friends. By November 1, I am nearly done with my shopping!" That means plenty of time for enjoying the real highlights of the season: Time spent with friends and family, making delicious baked treats, going to tree lightings and music events, even donating time at charities.

For a Rich Life . . .

LET GO OF THE "PERFECT GIFT" IDEA

How much have you spent over the years trying to outdo yourself or others on the "perfect gift"? As one Frugal Woman found, maybe you need to remind yourself that it is the thought that counts. She explains: "For me, the biggest step in finding frugal gifts was to get rid of the idea that I had to find the 'perfect gift' for each person on my list. I spent a lot of money trying to get just the right thing. But I realized eventually that there is no perfect gift. Anyone on my shopping list is perfectly able to go out and buy what he or she really wants. The purpose for me is not to give them what they have always wanted, but to offer some token of love or holiday spirit. When I started thinking this way, I cut down on the number of gifts I bought people, and what I counted as a gift. Now, homemade soup and bread go to just about everyone."

For a Rich Life . . .

GIVE GIFTS FROM THE KITCHEN

As one Frugal Woman notes, "Gifts created in your kitchen are a special way to share a little of yourself. It doesn't need to be elaborate or be made of costly ingredients. It should be a bit out of the ordinary and something the receiver is not likely to make. Try to match the gift of food to the food likes of the person who will receive it. Choose something that you'll enjoy making, or something that you and your children or grandchildren could make together. The way the gift is presented can be almost as important as the food itself. It's nice to use a container that will be used after the food in or on it has disappeared. Flea markets and yard sales are great places to shop for these kinds of giveaway containers."

Here are some other "from the kitchen (and heart) of . . ." ideas to try.

Gourmet Mixes

"You can make your own bean soup kits for a fraction of the price of the ones they sell in gourmet food stores. Choose a favorite bean soup recipe, then multiply it by the number of people you want to give small gifts to. Buy the ingredients in bulk at the local natural foods store. Split up the ingredients for each batch and seal them in zipper-top plastic bags. Tie each bag off with a pretty ribbon. (Recycled tomato sauce jars or mason jars work well too.) Print out the recipe for making the soup on labels on your computer and stick them onto the front of the plastic bag. My kids loved helping me mix up all the ingredients and measure them into the individual bags."

— ◆ —

TURKEY NOODLE SOUP MIX

A soup mix is a welcome gift during the holiday season, when there is usually plenty of leftover turkey meat on hand.

¼ cup red lentils

2 tablespoons dried onion

1½ tablespoons chicken-flavored bouillon granules

1½ teaspoons dried dill weed

⅛ teaspoon celery seed

⅛ teaspoon garlic powder

1 small bay leaf

1 cup uncooked medium egg noodles

Layer ingredients in a glass jar in the order listed. Cover the lid with a round or square of fabric that is cut 2½ inches larger in diameter than the top of the jar, fasten with a rubber band, and tie with ribbon to cover rubber band. Attach a gift tag with the following instructions for the recipient:

Turkey Noodle Soup

This makes about 10 cups of good, hot soup perfect for a cold night. Here's how to make it.

8 cups water

1 jar Turkey Noodle Soup Mix

One 10-ounce package frozen mixed vegetables

2 cups cooked, diced turkey or chicken

In large saucepan, bring water to a boil. Stir in soup mix. Reduce heat to medium-low, cover, and simmer 15 minutes. Discard bay leaf. Stir in frozen mixed vegetables and cooked turkey. Cook 5 minutes longer or until noodles and vegetables are tender.

"Create your own homemade baking mixes. Put the mix in a mason jar, a tin coffee can, or any type of container that seals and can be decorated. Stir together all of the dry ingredients (for cookies, muffins, quick breads, biscuits, or whatever) and put them in the decorated container. Print the directions on cute computer paper or write them on pretty tags. You've just created a gift that would cost twice the price at those specialty gift shops."

Bread and a Board

"This is a great 'new neighbor' gift. Bake a quick banana bread and buy a small cutting board with a handle. Put the loaf on the board, and wrap with colored cellophane and a ribbon."

Goodie Buckets

"Make a pretty bucket of baked goods. Buy a bunch of gallon-sized aluminum paint buckets from the department store. Use a hot-glue gun to attach half-inch-thick batting and line the buckets. Buy some holiday-themed fabric (1.5 yards will line six buckets), finish the edges on the sewing machine, and use the hot-glue to attach the fabric inside the bucket. Buy some simple, quarter-inch-thick ribbon and tie it around the rim of the buckets. Then bake until you can't stand to bake anymore and fill the buckets with holiday cookies. This project takes some time, but it won't cost you much. You can probably make 20 buckets in one weekend."

———— ✦ ————

"I am making chocolate-dipped pretzels. You can dip them in caramel, Rice Krispies cereal, chopped nuts, or just about anything. When cooled and dried, wrap them in cellophane and tie with ribbons for gift-giving."

———— ✦ ————

"My son recently moved out on his own so I am going to do a cookie-of-the-month thing for him. I will box up and send to him two or three dozen cookies every month. I will put them in reusable containers which he can always use (or return to me for more cookies)."

Family-Recipe Books

"I made a family-recipe cookbook last year for my oldest daughter. I used a journal that I picked up from the dollar store with a blank cover, painted a simple design with my acrylic paints, then wrote in the recipes. I added family quotes intermittently throughout the pages."

Breakfast in a Box

"Everything is so crazy on Christmas morning. A great, cheap gift is to make breakfast for a bunch of neighbors, especially those with small children. I get some cardboard box trays (the ones that hold soda cans at the supermarket work well) and fill them with different varieties of muffins, fresh fruits, quick breads, and more. You can buy muffins in assorted bulk packs at the price club for not a lot of money. My neighbors really look forward to their goodies."

For a Rich Life...

GIVE THE GIFT OF TIME

No, we're not talking about clocks and watches. In this busy world, sometimes all someone really wants (or needs) is a little extra time. Here are a few ideas for indulging friends and family with what they could need most.

Offer to baby-sit.

"For my sister who has found herself a single parent just before the holidays, I am keeping my nephew for sleepovers once a week. She gets private, sanity time, and shopping time without him underfoot, and I get to play 'best auntie.'"

Cook a meal.

"For my culinary-challenged sister, I'm offering myself for a night to prepare a romantic meal for her and her husband (and to clean up afterward, of course)."

Play cleaning lady.

"My friends and I are giving each other a 'spring cleaning.' We'll take turns—three of us will spend the day at the fourth friend's house, cleaning and organizing. (Besides, you always clean someone else's house better than your own.)"

The Frugal Woman Knows...
HOW TO WRAP THINGS UP

It's easy to spend as much—or more—on wrapping and decorations for gifts as on the gifts themselves. While many environmentally conscious Frugal Women use the comics pages from the newspaper or reuse beautiful paper saved from a present they have received (who wants to see more trees cut down?), there are plenty of other inexpensive and elegant wrapping ideas that will make your gift stand out in a beautiful light.

Make your own bows.

"Instead of store-bought bows, I use netting. It is inexpensive, can be bought at the fabric store, and a yard goes a long way. I cut the width I need to tie a bow and wrap it around the present like ribbon."

Collect decorations.

"Don't forget to collect pinecones, leaves, and branches with berries to decorate gifts. And check out the bulk section of the market for cinnamon sticks, candy canes, licorice whips (you can tie them into a bow), and other treasures."

Keep brown paper on hand.

"I keep a roll of plain brown craft paper in the house (about $4 for 50 yards). You can stamp or stencil designs on it and use it for wrapping presents. It looks great tied up with twine."

Use up that extra fabric!

"I have a lot of extra fabric around the house. So I thought, *Why not sew up gift bags instead of wrapping presents?* It helps me clean out my closets, and the bags will help keep extra trash out of the landfills. Plus, they can be reused. Teach your kids to sew and get them to help. The design is very basic, just like a pillowcase, and tied closed with yarn or ribbon. You can add some jingle bells too."

Make wine bags.

"Wine can be an affordable but thoughtful gift. A handmade wine bag makes it even more special. You can make four wine bags from one yard of fabric and some ribbon. Use a bottle to trace a pattern. The hem at the top should be wide enough to fit a ribbon through."

Reuse old ornaments.

"Old ornaments can be glue-gunned on the top of presents. Inexpensive yarn can be tied around the presents to add a homier touch."

Try feathers and shells.

"Feathers from the craft store and seashells (free) from the beach make great decorations for wrapped gifts."

Use funny photos.

"Here's an idea for affordable gift tags. Grab your box of I'll-put-these-in-an-album-someday photos (you know you have one) and find some funny family photos. Find one of your sister in her first bikini and tape it to her package. Find that picture of your brother doing a Blues Brothers impersonation and tape it to his present."

Recycle holiday cards.

"Take Christmas cards you received last year and cut tags from the fronts. Use the fancy scissors and cut out neat shapes, either those in the picture, or rectangles, ovals, etc. It's free—it only takes a little bit of time. Kids will have fun with this project."

RICH LIFE REWARDS:
A FRUGAL WOMAN'S TALE

Being frugal is a state of mind in which you make the most of what is valuable to you. For me it's being mindful of my relationship with my family: Taking care to honor commitments without overdoing it and forgetting about myself. Taking the time to give love and attention to those you adore. Not holding back in my pursuit of a spiritually rewarding life.

Frugality is about doing your best to learn from mistakes the first time and making smarter decisions the next time. I am trying to teach my children to contemplate their place in this world and leave it better than they found it. We each try and do what we can in a way that is special to us. I give what we really can do without to those who need it more than we do. We also recycle for a better tomorrow. We give of our time because it fills us with joy to know we may have made a difference to one person. Simple living is a conduit to a rich existence.

—Laura Dominguez-Marquez, Los Angeles, California

INDEX

✦

ABOUT THE EDITOR

✦

Stacia Ragolia is the vice president of community and services at iVillage. She and her family live in Westchester County, New York.

ABOUT *i*VILLAGE

✦

Based in New York City, iVillage Inc. was founded in 1995 with the intention of "humanizing cyberspace." In the early years of the Internet, there were few places for women to find solutions and discuss their problems, needs, and interests. By providing a clean, well-lit space, iVillage carved out a unique place where women could gather and find information and support on a wide range of topics relevant to their lives.

Today, iVillage is a leading women's media company and the number one source for women's information online, providing practical solutions and everyday support for women. iVillage includes iVillage.com, Women.com, Business Women's Network, Lamaze Publishing, the Newborn Channel, iVillage UK, Promotions.com, and Astrology.com.

iVillage.com's content areas include Astrology, Babies, Beauty, Diet & Fitness, Entertainment, Food, Health, Home & Garden, Lamaze, Money, Parenting, Pets, Pregnancy, Relationships, Shopping, and Work.

WHAT'S YOUR FRUGAL ADVICE?

♦————

Have advice on what the Frugal Woman should know for a rich life? We invite you to become part of our network of advice-giving women, and to have your words of wisdom featured in upcoming iVillage Solutions books, by sending your best advice on frugal living to:

iVillage Solutions Books
iVillage Inc.
500 Seventh Avenue
New York, NY 10018

Or write us by email at ivillagesolutionsbooks@mail.ivillage.com.

We look forward to hearing your advice, as well as any of your comments and thoughts about our books.